To Grace
with love
Christmas 1978
Phil.

WHICH ONE'S CLIFF?

WHICH ONE'S CLIFF?

—— THE AUTOBIOGRAPHY BY ——

CLIFF RICHARD

HODDER AND STOUGHTON

LONDON   SYDNEY   AUCKLAND   TORONTO

British Library Cataloguing in Publication Data
Richard, Cliff
    Which one's Cliff?
    1. Richard, Cliff   2. Singers – Biography
    3. Music, Popular (Songs etc.) – Great Britain
    – Biography
    I. Title   II. Latham, Bill
    784'.092'4   ML420.R5

    ISBN 0 340 23413 X (Paper)
    ISBN 0 340 23606 X (Boards)

Photoset and printed in Great Britain for
Hodder and Stoughton Limited,
Mill Road, Dunton Green, Sevenoaks, Kent
by Lowe and Brydone Printers Limited, Thetford, Norfolk

Contents

Photographic Acknowledgments

WHICH ONE'S CLIFF?

Introduction

FOR SOMEONE WHOSE pet hate is TV's 'This is Your Life', it might seem a bit inconsistent to be spreading my past over 192 pages of a book. For a guy still in his thirties, it even strikes me as a trifle presumptuous.

Yet here it is, a kind of literary 'This is your life, Cliff Richard', complete with a few long-lost relatives and hazy memories. All that's missing are the 'voices off' and Eamonn Andrews! Nevertheless, if it provides a fraction of the enjoyment of that top-rated TV programme, it will have been worth the slog.

Let me put the record straight right from the start, and shatter a few illusions. I didn't actually write the book – not physically, I mean. For starters, I'd never have found the time and, to be honest, I wouldn't have had a clue where to begin. When it comes to the chat, now that's different – I'll take on all comers. Wind me up and the chances are you won't get a word in edgeways. But put a pen in my hand and a sheet of blank paper in front of me and, apart from a few pathetic doodles, it'll be just as blank four hours later.

The truth about *Which One's Cliff?* is that Bill Latham actually did the work while I sat in the wings feeding the information. Technically, I think, you call it ghost-writing but, whatever it is, it worked, and I'm grateful to Bill for the leading questions and his ability to reduce tens of thousands of woffly words to something readable, and still manage to sound like me!

Now at last there's something in print which accurately and reasonably comprehensively brings together into context all the hundred and one reports and articles, features and gossip, which have circulated about my life and career and, more especially, about my Christian faith over the past eleven years or more. I say 'more especially' about my faith because there's no question about that being the factor which has towered over virtually everything I've done since the mid-'sixties. It's the reason, for instance, why I visited refugee camps in Bangladesh and travelled 300 miles in a Land-Rover over dirt tracks in the bush of Southern Sudan. It's the cause of past books like *Questions* and *The Way I See It*, for films such as 'Two a Penny' and 'His Land', and for hundreds of visits I've made in recent years to churches, colleges and schools throughout Great Britain.

I often wonder exactly where I'd be or, more important, *what* I'd be today if I hadn't become a Christian. It's one of those hypothetical questions and impossible even to hazard a guess at the answer. All I'm sure of is that personally, in terms of values, attitudes, priorities and relationships, there'd be a world of difference, and if this book achieves only one thing I hope it's to convince you that the Christian gospel was relevant and powerful enough to turn one modern life upside-down almost literally before your eyes!

Presumably no one writes a book about themselves unless they reckon their story's worth telling! I don't think I'm any exception, although if it were exclusively about me I'd have my doubts. Really this book is more about Jesus because it's His life – or rather a feeble reflection of it – that's being lived out in me. I hope that doesn't sound too pious. Maybe you'll need to read to the end to understand what I mean. I don't want to give the impression that this is some super-spiritual effort better suited to private devotions than an evening's armchair! It's about show-business and pop and Elvis and rock 'n roll. But even if I tried there's no way I can divorce that from Christ because, despite what some would have me believe, He's as much to do with music and entertainment and with TV and recording studios as He is with churches and Billy Graham.

This book's about all those things, each ingredient merging and overlapping and influencing the other to make one whole integrated experience. I've done my best to avoid spiritual jargon and clichés, and if I've failed here and there I rely on you to throw them out and do your best to see what I really mean. I've steered clear too of attempting any specialist in-depth pop history or analysis. I don't imagine the average reader would be that interested and, in any event, an objective 'neutral' student of the pop scene is probably much better suited for that kind of task.

Much of the early chapters are impressions which have stood out from a whole tangle of extraordinary fast-moving events, and we end where I'm at today – 'discovered' by America, wooed by the Russians, loving every second of my work, and looking forward to Jesus coming back.

Two thank-you's – firstly to Bill's secretary, Gill Snow, who faithfully hammered away at the typewriter hour after hour, and whose occasional discreet advice resulted in a bit of polishing here and there. And, secondly, to Hodder's Edward England for being so patient and understanding over deadlines and things!

Enjoy reading – and I'll see you around!

Cliff
OCTOBER 1976

There's nothing more relaxing than strolling the dog.

INSET The first time I ever sang in public was as Ratty in a school production of 'Wind in the Willows'.

1 Kites and Curry

TO THIS DAY I can't be sure whether monkeys swim under water. There was a lake where a bunch of us used to fish with old bent pins on bits of bamboo. We'd sit there and watch monkeys leap down from overhanging trees and crash into the water, holding each other's tails, like a great long string. They would all disappear and the next minute my cousin would yell that they were coming up on the far side. Whether they swam, or walked along the bottom, I've no idea but, sure enough, there they were – still holding tails, dripping wet, and loping off into the bushes. It's too vivid a memory to be a dream – I think!

I suppose I was five or six at the time, and the lake – or a big tank, I think it was – was at a place called Buxa, some miles outside Calcutta. India was home until I was seven, then Home Rule started and we left hastily, with little money and less dignity. I've been back just once. That was in 1973, on the way to Bangladesh, and there was nothing – no jolts of memory, no sense of homecoming, no emotion. It was another foreign country and all I felt was dismay at the mess that, in part, must have been our legacy. Today kids in Calcutta don't live, in our sense of the word. At best they exist in a kind of day-to-day survival exercise. Maybe the situation isn't that different. Maybe I was looking at the same scene through adult eyes. Maybe there was always disease and dirt and death and terrible poverty. If so, I don't remember.

India to me means kite-flying – not like we do it in England; in India it was a real art form. Kites there were made of tissue paper held taut by tiny strips of bamboo. There was no tail, just a piece of triangular paper at the bottom. The artistry came not so much in getting the thing to fly – that was simple – but in dive-bombing your opponent's kite. Even better was to cut through the enemy's cotton so that his kite zoomed off into the blue. The ultimate villainy was to give your own cotton a devastating cutting edge by soaking it in a mixture of finely-cut glass and egg-white. It produced a lethal weapon but it was considered 'fair do's' and my kite was generally regarded as a killer. The nearest we get to it here is conkers!

Life for the Webb family in India was happy and easy. Dad was area manager of a catering firm called Kelners, something like Lyons. They had the concession for Indian railways so he was out a fair bit, travelling around the country. We lived in the firm's apartment, a place with floors like great chessboards made of black and white marble. The best thing about it was that it was over the chocolate factory so sweets and cakes were easy to come by, through fair means and devious! Not surprisingly, gluttony set in at an early age and I've been plagued by it ever since. It was only when Minnie Caldwell in 'Coronation Street' referred to 'chubby Cliff Richard' that I took myself in hand and injected a bit of discipline into my eating habits.

One thing that had to go was condensed milk. My grandfather, who lived in Lucknow, where I was born, had an almost pathological weakness for it, which I either caught or inherited. My eldest sister, Donna, and I used to fight to scrape the tin but the ultimate ecstasy came years later when they put it in tubes and you could suck it out! A condensed milk sandwich, incidentally, has to be eaten to be believed!

More logical, I guess, is my passion for curry and rice. Again it's fattening and I daren't get stuck in too often but my mother makes one of the best and every so often, when there's no television or concert the next day, the diet goes to pot.

One of the few things I remember about school in India is having lunch brought in from home by our Indian cook-cum-bottle-washer, Habib. Along with dozens of other servants attending their respective Little Lord Fauntleroys, he used to carry platefuls of food, one on top of the other, all done up in a napkin with the four corners tied in a big knot on the top. We never knew what was in the napkin and lunchtime always held a degree of anticipation never quite matched in later years by school dinners in the canteen!

Most English people in India at that time were fairly wealthy. We had the best food, the best drink, and were waited on hand and foot. There was a woman called an ayah, who was a kind of nanny and washed and fed the children. Then there was a guy who swept up around the house and grounds, and two other servants who cooked and served the food. The most arduous chore for my mother was to decide what we'd have for dinner!

The Raj may have done a lot for India but there's little doubt that we took more than our fair share in return. I'm not knocking my father. He worked hard for his money and generally pulled his weight. Nevertheless, as I recall it, the whole system seemed to make use of a nation and its people primarily for its own ends.

Anyway, none of that bothered me as a six-year-old, and life was sunshine and playtime. St Thomas's Church of England School, just outside Calcutta, was in very spacious grounds, hemmed in by banana trees. I don't

remember learning much, although the botany lessons were fascinating. I think we called it 'Growing Things' – things like mango seeds which we embedded in blotting-paper soaked with water, stuck in a glass jar, and left nature to do the rest. The marvel of actually watching a 'thing' grow impressed me then and, nearly thirty years later, I'm still hooked. On my kitchen window-ledge at the minute there's a wrinkled avocado stone balanced on top of an old teacup, with its end just touching water. As yet there's no sign of life but any day now the shoot should appear and, with any luck, it'll be avocado salad for dinner next summer!

The only painful memory of school in India is having two front teeth yanked out. I'll spare you the details, but evidently they somehow got more permanently attached to the sleeve of another kid's cardigan than to my mouth. When eventually I grew new ones, they were better suited to a buck rabbit than to a small boy. There were no dental braces to help and all I got was my father's stern advice: 'Keep sucking them in, lad!' So keep sucking them in I did and, sure enough, it's left me with two good straight teeth and an annoying habit!

Just adjacent to the school was St Thomas's Church where I was a choirboy. I don't think I was a very good one as it was difficult for me – or anyone else, come to that – to distinguish one note from another. However, in red cassock and white ruff, I looked the part and, without being too cynical, I think that's what mattered. The whole family went to church every Sunday morning but it was principally a social affair – an occasion for mother to wear her best hat and to coo over her angelic son. I don't imagine there was much more depth to it than that.

Condensed milk grandad was one of a bunch of relatives who have taken on almost fictional Dylan Thomas-type qualities. Auntie Marge, for instance, was a spinster who baby-sat while Mum and Dad had the occasional evening out. I enjoyed Aunt Marge because she let me eat with my fingers. All Indians were skilled at it – a neat rolling of rice between the thumb and forefinger and then the deft flick into the mouth. It wasn't quite the done thing in nice circles of course, but Aunt Marge obviously didn't mix in nice circles and, as long as we didn't tell Mum and Dad, Donna and I were allowed to eat native. The only condition was that food went in our mouths and not down the walls. I suppose it wouldn't be quite the same with a prawn cocktail but I still prefer hands to cutlery, and when I went to Bangladesh recently I tried it again. It was like riding a bike: after nearly thirty years the roll-and-flick technique still worked and the food had that extra something. What I'd forgotten is that long finger-nails, necessary for guitar-plucking, get in the way and I spent the next couple of hours surreptitiously picking out rice grains!

ABOVE That's me, folks – front right, with the black jacket – terror of the Carshalton Sunday School.

BELOW Mum and my eldest sister, Donna.

Then there was Aunt Marge's brother, Uncle Tom. It could well be that I owe quite a deal to Uncle Tom for he was responsible for my first music experience. I use the term 'music' loosely for even Uncle Tom would have admitted that his voice was no great shakes. But at least he made a noise with his throat and the noise was accompanied by some enthusiastic guitar strumming. Mum said he sounded like Bing Crosby – that's about all she said and it's probably just as well for Mr Crosby could have sued for slander. But, for some reason I never quite fathomed, Uncle Tom was the black sheep of the family. He didn't come to our home much but his rare visits caused colossal excitement because we knew we'd end up at night with him sitting at the foot of the bed singing songs. Now there's something for the psychologists to get their teeth into!

But if Uncle Tom lit the first musical spark, Mum did her fair share to fan the glow. We had one of those wind-up phonograph machines with a built-in horn and one of my mother's party tricks was to tell me to go and pick out such-and-such a record. Now if I'd been twenty-seven at the time it would have been no great achievement, but I could hardly walk, let alone read. I think I must have memorised the colours on the labels because my success rate was well-nigh one hundred per cent. My favourite record apparently was 'Chewing a piece of straw' – surprising, really, that I've never recorded it!

My mother was always keen on records and in later years we'd listen avidly to the Top Twenty which, in those Radio Luxembourg days, used to be the result of sheet music rather than record sales.

But there were other things in India besides music to excite a little boy. Like the rioting just prior to Home Rule. Everyone else seemed terribly frightened by the gunfire in a nearby park but I revelled in it. This was better than Cops and Robbers. The whole business of hiding in a friend's house till the explosions had quietened down was pure adventure.

And then one day someone found a Moslem on the run from the Hindus holed up in a derelict garden just over the wall from our apartment. My father wanted to help the poor bloke out but, if we'd been discovered harbouring a Moslem, we'd have been putting our heads on the block. Every day for the best part of a week we lowered food to him over the wall as soon as it was dark, and when eventually we were positive that no one else knew he was there we humped him over to our side of the wall. Within minutes my father had whisked him away in a lorry, together with some of our Moslem servants.

One of the reasons, I think, why we were left more or less in peace at that time was the well-known fact that my father had been a keen hunting man in his younger days and kept a powerful gun in the house. At least, that's what they thought. In fact, the gun had been lost or stolen somewhere along the line and we were absolutely defenceless.

It became increasingly obvious to Mum and Dad that India was no longer a wise place to stay and when, during one festive occasion, coloured water, traditionally used to brighten up the fountains, was squirted at the white women, it was apparent that any last traces of respect had disappeared. The Webbs, together with thousands of other British families, were getting the big elbow!

But where to go? Dad was born in Burma, Mum had been in India all her life. It was a toss-up between Australia and Britain. Dad was all for Australia: he and a pal were set to start a business there, but Mum would have none of it. Our relatives were in England and that was that. My mother was, and still is, a strong-willed lady. I often wonder how things would have turned out if Dad had had his way. Twenty years ago, the opportunities for a pop-singing career in Australia were virtually nil. The record industry had hardly got off the ground. The likelihood of a Cliff Richard making any kind of impression was as probable as Mick Jagger turning his collar round.

But we plumped for England, sold up all we owned which, surprisingly, must have been incredibly little, and booked a passage on a boat. It really was as simple as that. There were no business complications, no strong emotional ties, no tears. Today, as I say, there's still no emotion. Certainly I want to be involved in some of India's problems but there's no real identification, no tugs at the heartstrings.

In a way I feel guilty about that because I know that many Indians feel a particular warmth and, in some instances, almost a reverence towards me. During a tour of South Africa with the Shadows, I remember going to a hotel cloakroom. There was an Indian shoeshine guy there who recognised me and literally threw himself at my feet and kissed them. To the Shads it was a huge joke and for weeks afterwards there was endless legpulling about 'my people'. For me it was an awful embarrassment and I've never quite learned how to cope with it.

The fact that someone who has made a name for himself internationally in entertainment should be born in India obviously means a great deal, and Indians by nature are exceptionally emotional and excitable people.

Just recently I received an invitation to take part in some Christian meetings in India and I'm really not sure about the wisdom of accepting. A regular secular-type concert would be fine but whether an Asian audience would be prepared to quietly listen to me talk about what I believe is another thing. I imagine that underneath would be a bubble of hope that 'perhaps he'll sing "Congratulations" or "Summer Holiday" '. I guess there's only one way to find out and I'll tell you the result some other time.

So, with the minimum of fuss, the Webbs upped and went, leaving behind the luxury that wasn't ours in the first place. After a three-day train journey to Bombay, we boarded the *SS Ranghi* which, we were told, was one trip away from the breaker's yard. At first it was ghastly. While Donna, who had been a very sickly child and had cost Mum and Dad a fortune in doctors' fees, loved every minute of it, I spent day after day stuck in my cabin being sick. Eventually I got some kind of puny sea-legs and discovered, just in time for the last lap of the journey, that cinema-shows on board ship were free.

I still can't take sea travel too happily and have a painful memory of a Channel ferry crossing not long ago in a Force 8 gale! And the jokers who claim the whole thing is psychological are talking through their hats. After two hours of misery in the gents' loo, the sickness and giddiness suddenly stopped. Seconds later there was a polite tap on the door. 'We're in the harbour,' said a voice.

The only notable event during the three-week voyage from India was that I learned to whistle. We were in the Suez Canal at the time and people on either bank, not much more than a stone's throw away, were sitting targets for piercing catcalls from lewd passengers lining the decks. It seemed good, safe enough fun, so I did what they did – shoved my fingers in my mouth and blew. The result was a totally new musical experience and a hefty belt round the ear from Dad.

Then suddenly we arrived at Tilbury Docks and I realised that England was a different colour. India was brown, England was green. We got in a taxi – Mum, Dad, Donna, baby Jackie, and me. We had a few suitcases, and Dad had five pounds in his pocket.

2 Family Ties

IF YOU'VE GOT to be the only boy among three girls, make sure you're the eldest! I have three sisters – Donna (or Donella, to be precise), Jacqueline, and Joan – and, as it was, I could lord it over them a bit. It would have been murderous if I'd been the youngest.

Actually my father, who I'll tell you more about in a minute, had drummed it into me never to raise my hand to a woman. There was a perfectly logical way round that! When Donna, my junior by just two years, used to drive me mad, I'd roll up a newspaper and wallop her with that. When mother came home and asked why Donna was crying, I'd say I didn't know, I'd never laid a hand on her!

Our experiences together as a family and our closeness, especially through some really hard times, still mean a lot. It's almost a cliché, I know, for people in the public eye to hark back to their inevitable childhood poverty. Maybe there is something in the theory that a tough start results in a greater determination to succeed. Personally I've never been aware of any kind of driving compulsion to 'prove' myself but, by any standards, those first three years in England were tough! I always get annoyed with people who look at me now and say, 'What do you know about the way the other half live?' The answer is, 'More than most.'

As soon as we set foot in the country with only five pounds in our pockets, life took on a very different complexion. The whole thing was a bit like Cinderella in reverse – comfort and being waited on like kings one minute; scrimping and dependent on the help of others the next.

At first my grandmother found us a room next to her in Carshalton. That room was our living room, bedroom, kitchen – the lot, and I remember my mother cooking porridge over a little green primus stove. I still love porridge!

After a year in Surrey, an aunt gave us a room in her home at Waltham Cross in Essex – but it was no bigger and the five of us went on living in each other's pockets.

My father, a terribly stubborn and independent man, hated the charity we had to accept from our relatives, and for him the council's decision to give us priority council-housing in Cheshunt must have been the sweetest relief of all.

But, oddly enough, it wasn't until we got our house that the seriousness of it all really got through. I guess that for Donna and Jackie and me there were plenty of preoccupations – school and friends and football and whatever the latest kid craze happened to be. But at Cheshunt our predicament immediately became more obvious. Furniture – or the lack of it – for instance. The first furniture we had was made from packing-cases which my father bought for a shilling each from the place where he worked. He brought two of them home and made our first chairs. We had those for years, even after I began singing, just as a sort of reminder.

And then I remember my mother crying a lot at nights – and no wonder. For her, the change of lifestyle must have been traumatic and there must have been times when it all seemed just too much. The whole business of bringing up a family, particularly if you're not very well off – the washing, the cleaning, the going out to work because father can't earn enough – all that was a horrific experience, coming from a situation where she could just snap her fingers and the food was brought and the chores done.

Yet somehow she coped, and I suppose that's largely why I admire her so much now. There can be few people who worked harder during that period than my Mum. Apart from looking after the kids – and just before moving to Cheshunt Joan was born – she would cycle six miles to work in the afternoon to save the bus fare, return about six in the evening and get dinner. She just never seemed to stop. I know many women who work just as hard but she had to adapt more than any of us and needed those extra resources of determination and courage. The amazing thing is that she has come through it all more or less unscathed and, although she is now over fifty, she is still mistaken from time to time for my sister!

Both she and Dad were pretty high-principled when it came to money matters, despite the lure of the 'never-never'. Although my father didn't earn much as a clerk and Mum's job was necessary to make ends meet, we managed very slowly to save a few pounds. Although we did buy one or two necessities on hire purchase, anything vaguely in the luxury bracket was carefully budgeted and saved for. Even the purchase of our beloved record-player was delayed until we had saved enough to buy it outright. It was a sound principle and one we stuck to for years. We didn't have a television in fact until my first record royalties had come through.

I suppose it's that background that makes me a little intolerant today of those who, at the slightest inconvenience, plead poverty and hardship and expect everyone to come running with extra bonuses, allowances or salary increases.

If a couple want to make a go of things, I reckon that in most instances they really can. It may mean sweat and a few tears but eventually they come through.

In the end our home was quite a nice council-house. There was no wall-to-wall carpet but we had decent furniture and a rug on the floor, and it was all ours.

I didn't realise how much I'd cared for my Dad until after he died, strangely enough. If someone had asked me as a boy if I really loved him, I would have thought twice before answering because I just didn't know. We weren't particularly close. He was very stern, always believed in using the rod, and very often did.

He was particularly strict about the time we came home at nights and woe betide Donna or me if we were as much as five minutes past the stipulated hour. One evening Donna and I had been to the pictures and we must have lost track of time. When we arrived back at the house after a leisurely dawdle, we looked at our watches and, to our dismay, found we'd overshot our limit by thirty minutes. And, sure enough, just as we'd been warned, the place was locked and bolted back and front, every room was pitch black, and there wasn't a key anywhere.

After initial panic, I had a brainwave. In the back garden was a coal-shed and in the coal-shed we kept an old pram that hadn't been used since sister Joan was a baby. It was filthy dirty, covered in coal-dust and cobwebs, but it was an object of refuge. In a gesture of manly gallantry, I told Donna to clamber into the pram, covered her over with my jacket and, when she'd snuggled down as best she could, I prepared to see the night out on the coal-shed floor alongside.

Ten minutes later, when the novelty was wearing distinctly thin and thoughts of hairy spiders, spooks and creepy-crawlies were taking on terrifying proportions, there were loud and purposeful footsteps outside. Dad had decided we'd learned our lesson, and two grubby and mighty relieved kids were marched to bed!

I don't know what the present child psychologists would have to say about discipline like that. Frankly, I couldn't give a hoot for their trendy 'do as you like' theories. I know he was right and only wish I could see something like it exercised today by Christian parents I meet in homes around the country. It's a sad indictment that some of the worst-behaved and disobedient children I've come across are those of Christian parents.

Of course, there are exceptions. I can think of a number of families where there's a tremendous, relaxed harmony and love and respect, and it's fabulous to spend time in their homes. But, as I say, sadly my over-all impression is of precocious little horrors who more or less rule the roost!

The point is that when you go into a Christian home you *expect* that much more – a generally higher quality of living and altogether better and more balanced relationships. When you don't find them, I suppose it's that much more apparent.

What causes the problem I don't know. Maybe it's the much-debated issue of parents being so busy with their 'Christian work', whatever it might be, that there isn't time to establish a proper base for wise discipline. On the few occasions when parents and children are together, Mum and Dad are reluctant to be too stern and little Johnny or Muriel are spoilt silly and get away with murder.

I know 'discipline' has all sorts of suspect connotations these days and some would confuse it with 'repression', but they're not synonymous in my vocabulary. Repression is something negative – not allowing for the sake of not allowing, whatever the situation – that's destructive and evil.

Discipline is about freedom and results from deep concern for an individual. God disciplines because He loves, not despite it. 'Freedom within the law' is a phrase I heard from somewhere and sticks in my mind. Certainly there's none without it, and the principle applies just as much to families as it does to society and the whole of creation.

Anyway, back to Dad! As I say, it wasn't his discipline that made communication difficult. One of the problems was that he never gave me the chance to do anything. If a plug had to be mended, for instance, I'd be the one who held the tools, while he did all the repairing! He seemed to be unable to really share and always wanted to do everything himself. Again, it was part of his incredibly wilful independence.

It sounds terrible but it wasn't until he fell ill and became more or less helpless that my opportunity came for being 'man of the house'. We got on a lot better as soon as Dad learned to relinquish a little of the responsibility.

Having got that off my chest, I must add that my father had as profound an effect on me as anyone else in my early life. For, in an off-beat, Old Testament kind of way, he demonstrated a faith in God which I am sure impressed me far more deeply than I knew at the time.

By an Old Testament faith, I mean there was little Christ-like gentleness or compassion about it – more the sternness one associates with fiery old prophets like Amos or Ezekiel. He never went to church – 'It's not for the likes of me,' he would say – yet praying was very much part of his routine. I remember he had this weird way of praying on all fours. I suppose it had something to do with him being in the Orient for so long, where it's usual for people to prostrate themselves before God. Often I would walk into his room and there he would be, crouching on his bed, on hands and knees. It all looked pretty fervent to me, although the prayers were never audible.

He always had a Bible in the house too and I remember two or three attempts to get us to read it together as a family, but the idea always petered out – probably due to our basic lack of enthusiasm.

People often ask whether my father was a Christian and I just don't know how to answer. Undoubtedly he had a faith in a God of justice, but I don't ever remember him talking to me about a Saviour or about a God who wanted to live His life in me, and that makes me think that his appreciation of the Bible was all rather lopsided.

It was only Donna and I who were old enough to have any kind of real relationship with Dad and it was this age proximity that brought us specially close together. Joan of course was really the baby – I was ten when she was born and we all spoilt her. Jackie was kind of middle-of-the-road – too young to be in our 'scene' but too old to be left too much out in the cold.

At the time I never realised how close Donna and I were because we used to fight tooth and nail regularly. It was a while later that Mum confided that Donna was my greatest ally. If Dad – or anyone else, come to that – was running me down, then Donna would be there to the rescue, saying what a great bloke I really was. The funny thing was that I used to do just the same for her. Behind the superficial cat-and-dog type relationship, there was a deep loyalty, and woe betide anyone who tried to threaten it!

Even allowing for my bias, Jackie must be one of the most sweet and gentle of people. She's always had a loving and sensitive nature and she's the last person in the world you would want to hurt. But Jackie is a Jehovah's Witness and, in the same way that I am not close to Hank Marvin who is also a JW, and in the same way that I can't be at one with anyone who doesn't share my faith, I suppose there had to be an intrusion even in a blood relationship. Much as we love each other and enjoy each other's company, I'm never totally free in Jackie's presence and vice versa. We are always aware that there is a certain area where we can't be completely close. One day I hope very much that we'll be able to shout 'Hallelujah' together. Maybe it won't be until we're with God in eternity but I guess we'll all be in for a few surprises then anyway!

At one point, Donna was on the verge of commitment to the Jehovah's Witness creed and it took near death to re-direct her. In 1973 Donna was critically ill and needed a blood transfusion. Because of the uncompromising JW teaching forbidding any kind of blood intake, based on what I'm in no doubt is wrong Bible interpretation, she adamantly refused the transfusion until she passed out. I don't know many people who follow through virtually to the death what they believe. Donna did, and for that she has my lifelong esteem. I don't know whether I could do anything like that if the test came, even if I thought it was right.

But the whole incident had tremendous repercussions, particularly for my mother. She was the one who made the decision: 'Do what you have to do to keep her alive.' Immediately the doctors went into action and gave her the blood transfusion. Today Donna is alive and well.

For Donna the experience meant some drastic reappraisal.

For my mother, who was a baptised JW, it meant being summoned before a JW 'tribunal'. But that extraordinary and slightly ludicrous 'trial' put the whole issue into perspective. A 'no' to the transfusion and Donna would be dead. God doesn't expect those decisions of us! Now my mother, although still JW-orientated, has discovered something new and dynamic from Scripture, as she's allowed the Holy Spirit to make the interpretations instead of the faceless *Watchtower* authorities.

Today the Webb family has gone its separate ways. My father died and my mother remarried. My sisters all married and are living in different parts of the country.

But there's still a bond between us and, as far as I'm concerned, it's quite unique and I love 'em all!

3 Then Along Came Elvis

THANK GOODNESS WE'RE seeing the end of the eleven-plus exam! If only its funeral had come twenty-five years earlier! I was one of the failures and at the time it shattered me. As a cocky little devil of ten, I was sure I'd pass. So were my primary school teachers in Waltham Cross. For two or three years I'd been the top boy in my class and we all thought the exam was a formality. Grammar school was just around the corner – literally and figuratively.

It had taken a couple of years and a good few nosebleeds to get used to school in England, anyway. At the start it was a nightmare. My first primary school was in Carshalton and all I can remember learning was how to defend myself. I suppose my skin was a bit swarthy after years in a hot climate and I was the target for endless taunts. 'Indibum' and then 'Red Indibum' followed me round every inch of the playground. Mum tried to help. 'It just shows how stupid these people are,' she said. 'They don't even know where Red Indians really come from.' Although I felt I was one up on general knowledge, I guess the sympathy didn't help much. But I must say I became a terrific fighter. I wasn't brave and I used to get away as often as not, but when I was cornered I gave as good as I got. My worst playground enemy was a kid who wore an old mac and looked like Batman, and whose chief pastime was to practise his wrestling holds on me. One day I couldn't stand it any more and I remember grinding his wrist hard into the tarmac. It was horrific really and I think I did him a good deal of damage.

And then there was the milk which was forced on us – nasty, white and cold! We'd never drunk it like that in India; there it was always hot with sugar.

The change-over from rupees to pounds, shillings and pence was another trauma. I had a terrible time and maths in school was a foreign language.

I hated England and everything about it for ages.

Then at Waltham Cross things became normal. My skin toned down to a pasty English white, taste-buds adjusted to cold sugarless milk and, although I trailed a mile and half behind in maths for the rest of my school career, I began to do pretty well in most other lessons. Then the big eleven-plus let-down. I reckoned that that failure permanently ruined my confidence in any kind of written examination. Even today I loathe exams and those kids' IQ tests still totally baffle me.

I always think there has to be some ulterior motive or trick – I don't know why. I've come to the conclusion that exams are virtually null and void anyway, because everybody who's proved himself as being educable during the year doesn't really need a test. Nobody who applies his academic qualities to his job is going to be tested – he just simply gets on with it. If someone can add two and two correctly during the year and you ask him to do it in an exam and he makes it five, it doesn't mean he can't do it, only that he's got exam nerves. There must be thousands of kids who fumble and fail crucial exams because of this anxiety business. There's that deathly silence, the woman who paces slowly up and down between the desks, and the regular change-over of warders. Psychologically it must be murderous – worse than the Eurovision Song Contest!

Maybe I'm just dimmer than most. All I know is that if you quiz me orally I'm in my element, and at least that's some consolation.

What made things even worse at that impressionable age of eleven was that when I finally went to my secondary modern school I was put in the middle stream. There was a lower, middle, and an upper, and I found myself in Middle C or something like that – pretty low down the scale, and among what I considered to be a lot of duffers from other schools in the neighbourhood. I was all set to hate school for the rest of my life, when, halfway through that first morning, a teacher – Mr Fade, I think it was – came into the classroom and announced: 'There's been a mistake. Is there a Harry Webb in this class?' I stood up, my heart beating like mad, and he said, 'You should be in Upper 1A!' I went to Upper 1A six inches taller and feeling that the world had paid me back a little of its debt!

I stayed in the A stream from then on and I never again had any kind of academic success. I didn't really enjoy learning; the only subject I was moderately good at was English Literature. I'm sure it was only because of Mrs Norris, my English teacher, that I stayed in the top stream. She reckoned that kids good at English had to be in the top class and I think that with her good reports I managed to scrape through.

If Basher Bates had had his way, I'd have been out on my ear very early on. Basher was the staff-room heavy. I have a vivid recollection of standing outside his room, freezing to death with fright, waiting to be whacked. Rumour had it that he carried up to eight canes up the sleeve of a withered arm, which suddenly found power to crash a stick on some offending victim. To our eyes he was a kind of Dracula figure and we all feared him like the plague.

People often ask me how I reacted to Religious Education in school. I must confess it meant absolutely nothing. It's unfair to blame the teacher, for he was snowed under by a dozen of us who really couldn't have cared less and who were determined to be bolshie. It was just a non-lesson and when O-levels came I deservedly failed!

It's ironic that a few years ago I seriously considered quitting show-business to take up teaching that very subject. I'll explain that rather embarrassing saga later. But it seems to me now that RE should be at the heart of so much of a kid's upbringing. To my mind, youngsters today are not getting the moral upbringing they should. That's a generalisation, I know, and probably sounds very pompous but it's what I honestly believe. Our society is suffering with a generation which is tending to throw out principles and morals which are basically good and, in my book, morality and spirituality go hand in hand. When human beings play at choosing what's moral, there's chaos. Everyone is right, no one is wrong. The speaker who dares to proclaim in public that this or that is immoral only earns for himself the label of 'reactionary' or, more likely, 'narrow-minded twit'!

For me, it's Godliness – I dislike the word 'religion' – that brings about a real morality, because it takes the choosing of what's good or bad out of the hands of man and puts it into the hands of God. And the Creator knows what's best for His creatures. His morality is about freedom rather than repression, health rather than disease.

School is a place of terrific influence. In Christian jargon, a great mission-field. However you describe it, more and more apostles of obscure and sometimes dangerous ideologies are realising the strategic value of the classroom as a place for effective communication and long-term influence. I would love to see Christian teachers, thousands of them, in primary and secondary schools throughout Britain influencing young people for Christ. I am not suggesting that they indulge in aggressive evangelism but simply that they be themselves and, through their attitudes and concern, show the appeal and reality of Christ. The principle of 'earning the right to speak' seems to be a crucial factor in any evangelistic effort.

Meanwhile, back in the Upper stream, I decided at fourteen to quit the Confirmation classes I was attending at the local C of E church. Again, it all seemed so tedious and irrelevant. Funnily enough, my parents did little to dissuade me and it was getting on for ten years before I set foot in a church again.

One of the priorities at that time was sport – although I reckon I reached my peak at fourteen! There was a fleeting achievement at soccer, when I played right-back for the Under-14 Hertfordshire Eleven; an even more fleeting craze for basketball, and a much more serious commitment to badminton.

Actually that's been my favourite game ever since, probably because it's the only one I can play with any degree of competence. I remember one of my managers telling me that badminton was a feeble game. It gave me great pleasure to grind him into the dust. He didn't realise how strenuous and how plain enjoyable it is knocking the daylight out of a bunch of feathers. I took it quite seriously for a time and my Dad and I made a formidable doubles team.

And I mustn't forget the javelin-throwing. Again, in my prime at fourteen, I set a school record which stood until just a few years ago. Either the wind was in the right direction at the time, or the school has had a remarkable succession of puny pupils!

But, in a class of its own – far, far more important than sport or anything else in school or out of it – was pop. And pop meant Elvis.

Until that landmark age of fourteen, pop music was only part of the background to things. Rosemary Clooney and Teresa Brewer were great but nothing to get that excited about. Donna and I enjoyed listening but that was all. It was music to fill a gap and when the Elvis era dawned it was as though a curtain fell and eradicated all the other stuff.

I don't think it's possible to analyse, other than technically, what was different. It's just that suddenly there was a raw natural music that people could relate to. In one sense it was a totally new style of music, yet basically the ingredients were very traditional music forms – rhythm and blues, black jazz from New Orleans, and country. The result of the mixture was rock 'n roll, and it was totally and fantastically different from anything that had come before. Both Donna and I were caught up in it from the start of the first beat of the first record we heard. All of a sudden life had a new dimension. We'd save like mad for an Elvis album and carry it home from the shop out of the wrapper, so all the world could see we were Elvis fans.

As soon as we got in from school, we'd have the record-player going and it stayed on till ten or eleven at night. I can't imagine how the neighbours stuck it, for the walls of the council-house were pretty thin and we played the music at full blast. Strangely enough, we had no complaints. Today, when I'm seriously listening to music, I still like it loud. Not so that it pounds your chest and hurts the eardrums, but loud enough to convey every instrument.

I guess it goes without saying that Elvis the performer was about as big an influence as his music. Like thousands of others, I'd spent hours in front of the mirror, miming to his records and polishing the movement.

The curl of the lip, the hip swivel, the gyrating legs – nothing escaped attention.

There didn't seem anyone else around to imitate. Even Frank Sinatra with his distinctive 'jazz' feel did nothing for me. I recognise now of course that he's technically a great singer – always spot on tune, with impeccable phrasing – but somehow there's nothing there that makes the hairs on my arms stand on end. Still, I suppose my stuff doesn't exactly get Frank hysterical. There's no accounting for taste!

My first public pop performance must have been at the Holy Trinity Youth Club Dance. I never sang solo at home – not that I was shy, but I always preferred to sing along with records and they were so loud no one could hear me. Then I branched out. We formed a group from school called the Quintones. There was Beryl Molyneux, Freda Johnson, John Vince, someone else – it could have been Betty Clark – and me. First, we sang in unison and harmonies and then I went into my big Elvis take-off with 'Don't Be Cruel' and 'Heartbreak Hotel'. Unaccompanied, of course. I tell you, at fourteen I was really into it. Nothing else mattered. Life revolved around the turntable.

It was about then that Dad bought our first guitar. A real duff one that cost about two pounds. I say 'our' guitar because it was as much for himself as for me. I knew that he'd played banjo in a trad jazz band when he was younger but I'd never heard him play till then. And really he was pretty good. He knew various chord progressions and did his best to teach me. There was G, C and D7, and you could sing almost anything to those basic sequences. I remember stuttering through my first self-accompanied solo: 'If I had the wings of an angel, over these prison walls I would fly.' It wasn't easy, rather like tapping your head with one hand and rubbing your stomach with the other, but co-ordination improved and, once I'd mastered two or three manoeuvres, we built on them, went on to another key and learned more chords. I'm not much beyond that today. Basically I still only strum, maybe with just a shade more competence, although that's debatable!

The first guitar which was actually mine was stolen before we'd finished paying for it. That was really disappointing. Again, Dad bought it when I was sixteen for twenty-seven pounds and on the last night of my first professional tour it was whipped from the stage-door at the Colston Hall, Bristol.

Today I suppose I react to Elvis the same way some of my fans react to me. I like the old stuff best. For my money, Elvis's later material doesn't stand comparison with what must be classic pop material. No one is going to sing my songs, for instance, the way they sing 'All Shook Up' or

Outside 'Graceland', Elvis's home in Memphis.

'Heartbreak Hotel'. Those were classic pop songs and we British never really competed. The Beatles in later years found their own niche in pop history but even their music was based on Elvis, Chuck Berry, Bill Haley, Jerry Lee Lewis and Little Richard, and they would be the first to admit it.

Let me digress for a minute, and admit to one of my biggest regrets – that I blew what was literally the one chance of a lifetime to meet Elvis. It was in 1976, while I was bombing round the States promoting 'Devil Woman' and the 'Nearly Famous' album, and someone in the business asked if I'd like him to fix a meeting. At the best of times I have an aversion to meeting famous people in contrived situations and, on top of that, I'd heard that Elvis at that period was grossly overweight and I wasn't keen to meet a grotesque fat man who might shatter all my hero illusions. I'd wait until some other time, I reasoned, until Elvis matched up to his image. With hindsight I realise just how daft that was. I would love to have met him – to have had the opportunity to assess him as a person, even if only to decide for myself that he was pleasant or aloof.

Now, like virtually everyone else, I can only base any judgment on the opinions and reports of others, and it's mighty difficult to discern between fact and fiction. Perhaps the nearest we'll get to the truth is told by Elvis's three bodyguards in the book that was written just before his death, *Elvis – what happened?* If you're prepared for shattered illusions, then read it. It's an object lesson about 'possessing everything yet having nothing'. Professionally Elvis achieved and deserved every accolade and every superlative in the book. He entertained, enlivened and enthused millions around almost the whole world. Yet at 42 he collapsed and died in his own bathroom, utterly alone – his metabolism unable to cope with life any more. In the most important area of all, Elvis failed. Relationships, real meaningful relationships, were non-existent and his perspectives were frighteningly irrational and distorted. The picture I get is of a naïve child treating everything in life as some sort of game – a game in which he really believed he had absolute command.

Strangely enough, I was warned about Elvis's death about a month or so before it happened. A much-respected friend of mine, Jim Collier, director of 'Two a Penny' and 'His Land', had heard that Elvis was seriously sick – physically as well as mentally. 'Don't be surprised' he told me, 'if Elvis dies within the next two years. His body can't take much more of what he's giving it.' At the time I remember expressing a rather stunned disbelief and then discounting the whole thing, like most of us do with predictions that are unpalatable and hard to grasp.

When the news broke, there was obviously a good deal of confusion surrounding what actually happened. Reginald Bosanquet, I think it was, on 'News at Ten' first reported that Elvis was dead but then, moments later, made a correction. Latest reports were that he had collapsed, been taken to hospital, and was under observation. I went to bed that night believing that that was actually the situation. I could not accept for one second that Elvis Presley could possibly be dead. For a start, he was only five years older than me. But Jim Collier's words the month before were niggling.

At 3 am the telephone rang. It was LBC – the London Broadcasting Company – 'What was my reaction to Elvis's death?' Half-asleep, I told them that they must have got their facts wrong: Bosanquet had said that he was only in hospital.

The truth dawned very slowly. I don't recall what I said in the middle of the night – only that I prefaced every comment by '*If* this is true . . .' and '*If* you're right . . .'. It must have sounded odd when transmitted later that morning.

Nowadays I still often sport an Elvis lapel badge somewhere on my shirt or jacket and I'm proud to be known anywhere as a discerning fan. Rock and roll will continue to be performed, sometimes better than Elvis did it, certainly as well, by many other artists. But no-one will ever replace him as the figurehead. Elvis was and still is rock and roll – the epitome of what it's all about: hip-shaking, leg-swivelling and gutsy: white people trying to do black music and, what's more, doing it successfully. Together with Bill Black, DJ Fontana and Scotty Moore, Elvis was the great innovator – the guy, if you like, who invented the whole pop/rock scene.

I asked someone recently what it was like to see Elvis perform in his later years. 'Sure, he was fat' was the answer, 'but it was Elvis, the man who began it all – and that's what mattered.'

I'll save a detailed tribute for some other context. At the moment I'm well aware that if there were no Elvis, there would be no Cliff Richard. Personally, he mattered *that* much.

But back to adolescence and to things that mattered a whole lot less – like Bill Haley getting me stripped of my prefect's badge. I'd been one of those terrible kids who spent hours queueing for tickets to see him perform when I should have been at school. As a punishment my prefect's badge was taken away and all the privileges that went with it. 'In ten years' time you'll have forgotten Bill Haley completely,' said Jay Norris, my English teacher. Ten years later, Bill Haley came to London and I remembered her prediction. With the faintest of smirks and a box of chocolates, I was delighted to tell her that for once she was wrong!

Strangely enough, school meant much more to me after I'd left than while I was a pupil, and the influence of friends whom I met there has been responsible for much of what's happened in my life these last ten years.

Looking back now, I realise that the start of a long chain of events was during my O-level year. The exams were futile but the people around me were great. There was a group of us who somehow jelled together in a remarkable way and even Jay, who that year became a friend as well as a teacher, says it was one of the best class/teacher relationships she can remember. I guess that's borne out by the fact that several of us still meet quite frequently and only recently we did a kind of reunion production at the school.

We chose *Midsummer Night's Dream* and I was Bottom. The cast was made up of past and present pupils and staff and, although it was my first attempt at Shakespeare in front of a paying public, it was one of the most enjoyable things I've done in my career. The enthusiasm from everyone concerned was something you don't always find in professional productions and, on top of that, I had the chance to do something 'cultural', be involved in teaching kids to enjoy Shakespeare, and meet people I hadn't seen since schooldays. As adults, they could see through all the 'fakism' of show-business and we were able to pick up friendships where we left them as kids.

In fact I'd never have known most of those people if I'd left school immediately at fifteen. That's what I'd wanted. For years I'd been counting the days but when the time came I hadn't a clue what to do. I wasn't good enough at any one thing to go in for a specialist career, so I was more or less relieved to take Mum and Dad's advice and stay on for another year and a half for O-levels. It was a useful breathing-space – eighteen months to put off the decision about a job. The O-levels were almost incidental. The miracle was that I passed English Language. I'd expected to pass in Literature but no one gave me a dog's chance in Language. But then I've told you what I think about exams!

And all the time there was this burning urge to sing, to get out there on stage and be like Elvis. But in a council-house in Cheshunt, it just seemed a futile dream.

4 Exit Harry

EVERYTHING HAPPENED SO quickly after I left school. Within a year, I'd signed a professional recording contract and there were concert tours, television, films, and Cliff-mania. The details of all that happened seem blurred round the edges now, even though I've trotted them out to hundreds of reporters around the world, who never seem to tire of ancient history. Certainly the late 'fifties and early 'sixties was a remarkable period of musical upheaval and I sometimes have to pinch myself to make sure I really was part of it. But I'll leave it to the experts and objective observers to give their in-depth assessments. I must confess that sometimes the serious analyses sound all too presumptuous, as we read into situations rhymes and reasons that were never there.

They called my first job 'Credit Control Clerk' but forgot to mention the tea duties. The latter I did well, the former disastrously. My grasp of English geography was pretty duff and the job involved sorting out accounts into regions – Northern, Midlands, South-west and so on. When I tell you that only a year or two ago I twigged that Cornwall wasn't part of Wales, you'll appreciate why I didn't excel. It was a ghastly twelve months and, to make things worse, I bungled it under Dad's very nose. It was he who got me the job with his firm, Atlas Lamps, hoping, I suppose, that I might show a flair for executive management. What a joke! Each morning we cycled together the eight miles to work, each day we sat at opposite ends of a big open-plan office, only communicating at tea-breaks and lunch-hours. And each evening we pedalled back home, weaving in and out of rush-hour traffic. It was unrelieved boredom. I don't blame Atlas, but why they put up with me for twelve months I can't imagine. The fault was mine. I've always found it impossible to give any concentrated attention to things which don't interest me, and I just couldn't have cared less about bulbs, accounts or executive management. All that mattered was music – rock 'n roll music especially – and the fact that listening and singing had to be confined to evenings and weekends made it all the more magnetic.

A rare bus-ride to work one morning got things moving. Call it luck, coincidence or fate if you like but, looking back now, it's hard to put it all down to random chance. I found myself sitting next to a girl who was an old classmate. We got chatting and apparently her boyfriend, Terry Smart, a drummer in a local skiffle group, was looking for a vocalist. She remembered my Elvis take-offs at school and suggested I get in touch. I did, with the result that for two months I sang a folksy style of stuff which, although never appealing personally, was a step in the right direction. Both Terry and I were rockers at heart and after a while we decided to quit the skiffle scene and set up our own rock'n roll group, the Drifters. I suppose in a way we'd already made a name for ourselves around Cheshunt and Waltham Cross, so there was no problem in getting bookings. Youth clubs, Saturday evening dances, and then one night 'big time' at The Five Horseshoes in Hoddesdon. We were given space at one end of the bar and, to the accompaniment of friendly chatter, the chink of glasses, and the occasional hiccup, we belted out our repertoire. In retrospect, we were pretty awful, but no one protested and for our pains we were plied with occasional shandies and whatever silver was in the till at the end of the day. That usually meant a pocket of half-crowns each. The Atlas wage packet was fatter but there was no doubt which gave me greater pleasure.

There were four of us in the Drifters then – Terry, myself, Ian Samwell, who seemed continuously on leave from the RAF, and Norman Mitham. There was no bass guitar and, considering that that's the instrument which gives any group its gutsy sound, it was an odd omission but, as I say, we got away with blue murder.

To this day I'm not sure whether Johnny Foster was totally tone-deaf, a fortune-teller, or a brilliant spotter of potential. Maybe he had to be all three. Whatever he saw in us, his offer to be our manager sounded like an hysterical joke. I'm not sure now what John did for a living; he certainly wasn't in show-business and his approach at The Five Horseshoes may have been prompted by a double brandy, for all I know. But he was genuine, absolutely convinced that stardom was round the corner, and just as naïve as we were. And it was because of that, not despite it, that this burly genial character succeeded beyond any of our most extravagant dreams.

What we are, what we do and where we do it is determined largely, I believe, by the people we meet and by the friendships which result. Johnny Foster was one early key figure and I owe him a lot. From the start, it was clear John was a go-getter. Somehow he fixed us a week at the famous Two I's Club in London. I kind of expected that Lionel Bart or someone associated with the place at the time would come in and say, 'This kid's going to be great!' and make us stars overnight. After all, it happened that way for Tommy Steele and Terry Dene. But not a bit of it. The audience was blasé and the wage just about covered a late-night taxi home.

But John was determined and very shrewd. His master-stroke was spotting a poster advertising a talent contest at the Shepherd's Bush Gaumont. The idea was that we should offer ourselves, not as competitors but as free *top-of-the-bill* artists. That was the genius – it was top-of-the-bill or nothing – and the psychology worked! The management jumped at the something-for-nothing offer and there we were, on stage in a London theatre, coming on to close the show to a packed house. It didn't matter that the audience was made up mainly of kids and that it was Saturday morning. It was a fabulous experience! When you work in dance-halls and pubs, people aren't bothered with who's doing the playing. The music's important but anonymous. Saturday morning at the Shepherd's Bush Gaumont was the first time people had actually sat down in rows to watch us. We went out as brash as could be, did the Elvis and Jerry Lee Lewis stuff, and got screamed off the stage. It was an incredible, fantastic reaction, and the feeling was new and marvellous.

About a month later, we went back, again for nothing, only this time John persuaded a London agent called George Ganjou to watch. The reaction was the same. Everyone screamed – except George. The act did nothing for him. But we'd come prepared. A few days earlier we'd recorded a demo disc at the HMV store in Oxford Street. It cost us five pounds but what an investment! We gave the disc to George, who promised to play it to no less a recording man than Norrie Paramor of EMI. George kept his promise, although Norrie confided later that an opera singer had stolen the limelight and the Drifters' disc was almost forgotten. However, on the strength of that recording – 'Lawdy, Miss Clawdy' and 'Breathless' – Norrie asked us to audition. Studio 2 at EMI, Abbey Road, St John's Wood, was the venue – a place I've grown to know inside out over the past eighteen years.

On that first visit we were sick with nerves. Everything, it seemed, depended on whether this softly-spoken A & R man liked what we did. If he didn't, it was back to The Five Horseshoes; if he did . . .

I guess you know the outcome. We did our stuff and, amazingly, Norrie, bless him, was impressed. We passed the audition. A record contract was on its way.

By this point, incidentally, I'd quietly but effectively got rid of Harry Webb. Can you imagine it – Harry Webb and the Drifters, or later Harry Webb and the Shadows? Neither could I. Somehow Harry didn't have a hit parade ring. The image was all wrong. We needed something more sophisticated, a simple name, but sufficiently different to make it stick. For hours we concocted hundreds of exotic-sounding names until eventually

ABOVE One of my early duff notes! Sharing the pain is Norrie Paramor, who for nearly fifteen years was my recording manager.

BELOW Part of the early line-up with Bruce, Hank, and Jet Harris.

One of my favourite cars was the Chevrolet
Corvette Stingray.

My dad and I ⟩
quite a formida⟩
badminton do⟩
pair.

we arrived at Russ Clifford. From there, we ventured to Cliff Russord and, after a thumbs-down on Russord, Richards was suggested. Then came more brilliant applied psychology, this time from Ian Samwell. 'If you drop the "s",' he reasoned, 'and make it Cliff Richard, people are bound to get it wrong, and you can make a point of correcting them. Then, on radio and TV, you'll get the name mentioned twice.'

You'll understand we were thinking big at the time, but he was perfectly right. I've lost count of how many times the trick worked in broadcast interviews. Today I still get letters from my record company even, addressed to Cliff Richard*s*, and there are a dozen awards at home made out to the wrong chap!

Family reaction to the change of name was almost uncanny. I announced one evening that from now on I wanted to be called Cliff, and that was that. Occasionally over the breakfast table my sisters would slip up and ask Harry to pass the cornflakes, but then they'd be terribly apologetic, as though it really mattered.

The only occasion I use my real name now is on certain legal documents, although my passport allows the compromise: 'Harry Webb, professionally known as Cliff Richard'. But, apart from the signature, Harry has long been forgotten by all except schoolfriends and fakes. Returning to Cheshunt recently, it was fabulous to have old teachers calling me Harry – that's how they remembered me and why should they change? The fakes assume that Harry is the 'in' name, restricted to family and close friends. It's a real giveaway. One of them 'phoned the Palladium; it was my sister, the caller said, wanting to speak to Harry. I didn't bother to take the call.

When we got the green light for recording, it was obvious that our ordinary jobs had to go. For me that was no hardship at all. For nearly twelve months, my body had been in one place while my mind and interest were elsewhere. 'Good luck,' they said at Atlas. 'We know we're not suited!' Two weeks later, on August 9th, 1958, I turned professional. Already we were learning some of the realities behind show-business glamour. Johnny Foster had fixed a gig for us in a small dance-hall somewhere up north. The show ended and we'd nowhere to stay. We couldn't afford a hotel so that hall manager let us sleep on benches on the dance-floor. But the gig was worth ten pounds and that was comparatively big money.

The release date for our first record was August 29th. The A side was to be a song Norrie found, called 'Schoolboy Crush' and the B side featured a hastily put together Ian Samwell composition, 'Move it'.

Waiting was agony but a short season at Butlins in Clacton gave us something to do and provided good performing experience.

Again we used our 'Let's be different' technique. The management wanted us to wear the Butlins redcoat outfit, the same as a hundred and one other people in the entertainment section. 'Didn't they realise we were special?' Johnny argued. We had to have something distinctive. We got it: white shirts with a huge red V on the chest – no one else on the camp had them. We were instantly recognisable and again it worked. I don't think it was conceit or arrogance on our part. Admittedly, we wanted to be special – not that we were, but we thought we should be. It's important to hit the balance, to know that, on the one hand, you're nothing out of the ordinary in terms of humanity but that, on the other, as stage performers, you're automatically set apart by the audience, whether you like it or not. Always, I've felt, it's professionally justifiable to underline that separation in the things you say, do and wear. But I'll tell you later how I've had to temper that view since I became a Christian.

At first, Butlins was one drama after another. They put us initially in the Calypso Room, a gentle sophisticated sort of nightclub, featuring a Hawaiian band. Unleashing us in an atmosphere like that was disastrous. Next morning we were hauled before the management who told us very politely that they didn't think we were quite suited to the Calypso Room, and would we transfer to The Pig and Whistle? We were used to pubs, but sadly the Pig and Whistle clientele weren't accustomed to us. The blend of alcohol and rock 'n roll was rather too heady for some, and smashed tankards and overturned chairs meant another morning interview with the management. This time we were directed to the Rock 'n Roll Ballroom which – surprise, surprise – was just right. There were two stints – a painful half-hour morning bout and a more civilised evening concert. Those mornings really were a struggle and ever since I've ducked any sort of singing performance before midday. It's part-psychological, no doubt, but I know for a fact that my voice needs longer to wake up than the rest of me. But try telling that to the vicar who 'only wants one song' during morning service!

The rest of the time at Butlins was like holidays with pay and last thing at night the ultimate in luxury – doughnuts and Horlicks.

The record release was a non-event really. The date came and went and there was nothing – no rave reviews, no overnight million seller. We returned from Butlins and waited. I wondered whether Atlas would take me back. Maybe I could swot up and learn whether Manchester and Newcastle were south-west, north-east or wherever.

I didn't have to. One day Johnny Foster arrived at our Cheshunt council-house, nearly purple with excitement. 'You'll never believe it, we've got a tour!' he announced. 'Guess how much?' We guessed.

Twenty-five pounds a week? Fifty pounds? Sixty pounds? At £100 we gave up playing it cool. Johnny told us – £200. Till then fifteen pounds had been top whack. Delirium took over.

As one of EMI's new artists, we were being put on the road in a kind of variety show with the Kalin Twins as top of the bill. This was a new league altogether and gradually the truth dawned. Our line-up, as it was, was awful. We urgently needed a bigger sound and more talented musicians, and that was the cue for Hank Marvin and Bruce Welch to step into my life.

Johnny came across Hank playing at the Two I's. 'He looks like Buddy Holly and plays like Ricky Nelson's guitarist,' he reported. Sure enough, he did, and Hank was willing to join us on tour on condition that his friend, Bruce, who played rhythm guitar, was taken on too. Right from the start, it was terrific. Hank had this great rock 'n roll feel and, with his Buddy Holly looks, and my Elvis impersonation, we couldn't fail. In fact Hank really landed on his feet and turned out to be the rich man of the tour. Already he had earned himself a reputation as guitarist from the Two I's and was snapped up by other artists on the bill to help out on their accompaniment. Mickie Most, who was then part of a duo called the Most Brothers, paid him, the Kalin Twins paid him, and I paid him. No wonder he's been around ever since!

Three things happened about that time which combined to give what I suppose must be one of the most spectacular launchings to any showbiz career. There was the tour, a TV show and the record. Together they got me off to a storybook start that no present-day million pound promotion machine could match. In our day there wasn't that kind of money about, nor the kind of American tycoon outlook that was prepared to create a star or concoct an image. But fortunately television and records were enough. Television, which meant producer Jack Good, and records, which were Norrie – they made my career for me. They made it, they didn't buy it.

The TV thing got off to an embarrassing false alarm. 'Six-Five Special', a 'fifties version of 'Top of the Pops', asked us to audition on the strength of the new record, which still hadn't sold beyond the record shops in Cheshunt. After a couple of numbers we were stopped and told, with brutal frankness, that our style was neither new nor likely to last. One of the floor managers discreetly held the door open for us!

That might have been our first and last TV experience, were it not for Jack Good, from the rival channel's 'Oh Boy' programme. Now Jack is another of those early prominent influences who steered me in a direction which paid off handsomely. Jack was totally sold on 'Move it' which, remember, was the B side of our single. That's the number, he insisted, that I sing on the show. 'Schoolboy Crush' was out.

Now Jack Good was a man to be reckoned with in the pop world at that time and EMI didn't think twice about a change of campaign. Virtually overnight, advertisements were re-worded and 'Move it' became Cliff Richard's first A side.

Jack's advice to me was more radical, and verging on the blasphemous. 'Quit the Elvis impersonation.' If it had been anyone else, I'd have given him a coarse answer, but I listened and did as I was told. Off came the sideburns, away went the guitar, and I was left in front of microphones and cameras with no props, feeling half-naked, and with no Elvis image to hide behind. The whole thing was terrifying, but ridiculously easy. There was no need to be Mr Personality – Jack wanted just the opposite.

I stood there waggling one leg, my arms down at my side, desperately trying to keep them still, and curling the lip whenever I thought of it. Smiling wasn't permitted at any point and that was a relief. I'd always been terribly self-conscious about a tooth which was smaller than the rest and slightly ingrowing. When I smiled, it looked a cross between a fang and an injury. As soon as I could afford it, I had it capped.

The image was meant to be mean and sour, and the outfit I wore matched perfectly. A pink ill-fitting long teddyboy jacket, black shirt, black trousers, pink tie, grey suede shoes and, best of all, pink luminous socks. Ludicrous as it seems now, that was my stage uniform for nearly three years and every Cliff Richard impersonation thereafter bore the trademark.

I also suffered a plague of luminous socks. They poured in by every post; the manufacturers must have netted a fortune. Yet, despite all the careful preparation, that first 'Oh Boy' appearance didn't rouse a murmur. Marty Wilde got screams, I got genteel applause. A newspaper review the following day didn't mention my name but referred to 'a sour-faced young man, apparently chewing gum'. That was me singing!

Then, suddenly, 'Move it' made the charts and everything changed. Three or four weeks later, I did 'Oh Boy' again and I couldn't hear myself sing for the screams. I wore the same outfit, sang the same song in the same scowly way. One week nothing, the next I was nearly torn to bits and couldn't get out of the studio. It was unbelievable and it taught me that kids simply scream at who they choose. No artist can manipulate an audience if it doesn't want to be manipulated. I've often had people compliment me after a show for having the audience eating out of my hand. OK, so I did, but they wanted to be fed, they wanted to be taken along, and if you have the personality that they latch on to they'll be taken anywhere. I was fortunate to learn that early on, and it helped me to see what was happening in better perspective.

The success of 'Move it' meant a similar phenomenon during the Kalin

Twins' tour. That threw me for the first time into show-business politics. At the commencement of that tour, the Kalins' current release was top of the hit parade. Halfway through, they dropped to ninth place and we leapt to second. Consequently, every night the boys and I were stopping the show. Our spot came after the interval, immediately prior to the Kalins' act, and there wasn't a single night that those lovely people didn't have to battle through chants of 'We want Cliff'.

Like most business, showbiz has its cut-throat tactics and when we were asked if we'd move our act to an earlier spot we refused. Our contract said we would open the second half and we were sticking to it. Professionally it was the right thing to do, of course. All the publicity about a new singer eclipsing the Kalins couldn't have been better or more timely.

I had my eighteenth birthday towards the end of that tour and we were playing the De Montfort Hall, Leicester. It was an emotional time. The stage was strewn with flowers and the whole audience got up and sang 'Happy Birthday'. You can't imagine the feeling – to be on your first tour, with your first record just happening, and this kind of incredible reaction. Financially, too, the tour was a roaring smash and, before the last night, promoter Arthur Howes had plans for further touring, this time with 'Cliff Richard and the Drifters' new top billing. Little did I imagine then that nearly twenty years on Cliff concerts would still be filling halls around the country and we'd be running our own promotion agency.

OVERLEAF, ABOVE For about ten years Jan Vane ran the UK fan club.

BELOW Only a few of us left! Adam Faith's career took a different direction.

RIGHT One of the best-dressed acts of the fifties!

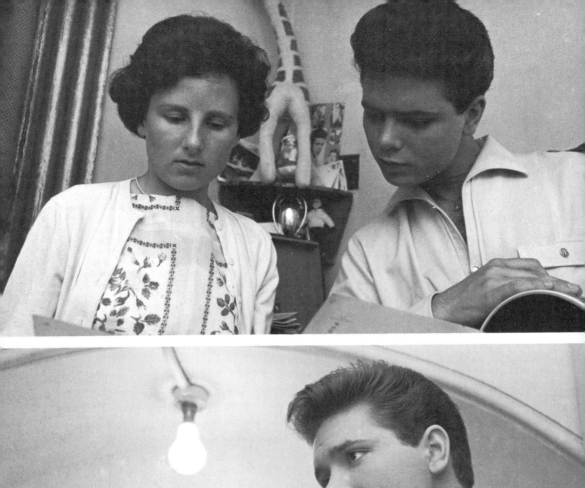

5 Lift-Off

'IS THIS BOY too sexy for television?' ran a huge centre-page headline in the *Daily Mirror*. 'Britain's bad boy of pop,' said another. 'Is he a bad influence on your daughter?' I can't help chuckling at those old cuttings now for the act was so schoolboyishly naïve. Of course I played for screams. It was fantastic to go on stage, look sour, shake a leg, and hear the place erupt. But as for being directly sexual, that was journalists' licence. It made the story worth reading and, in the early days, we were happy to go along with it.

Whereas today the pop scene is packed with groups and solo artists, most of whom are far more musically talented than we ever were, I was leading a very limited bunch in the late 'fifties and had the dubious pleasure of full press attention. Tommy Steele was there too of course and for a while was also daubed with the same sex image. But Tommy was never completely at home with rock'n roll and wisely moved on to something which better suited his talents. Marty Wilde was another contender but, for some reason best known to the record-buyers, I won. I recently saw a couple of 'Oh Boy' shows, dug up from the archives, and Marty was terrific. He looked good, sang brilliantly, and was way ahead of his time. That, I suppose, is the answer because following Marty was a greasy little kid with a nondescript voice, who was being acclaimed 'Britain's golden boy of pop'. As they say, it's a funny old business.

I mentioned earlier that it's the public who decides whether or not they want to scream at any particular artist and, once I'd grasped that, the danger of believing that I was God's gift to show-business never seriously got in the way. At the same time, I was surrounded by sane level-headed people who would have let me know in no uncertain terms if I'd started throwing my weight about. I never was, and never have been, encircled by fawning yes-men. They're around in our profession but I'm thankful they've never been around me, because they can make you believe you're something you're not.

In the early days Dad was about too, and his restraint and his down-to-earth good sense were invaluable. At first there was a bit of tension because Dad wanted to be closely involved in management. But it's like your wife or husband teaching you to drive – it rarely works, and in

Don't laugh! In 1959 they actually took it seriously.

this instance it would have been just too difficult to say 'That's wrong, Dad'. But he took it well and always remained very interested in all that happened, and wanted to vet every contract and every new plan. Most of all, though, his concern was for me. On one occasion I was really under the weather and had television, stage shows, recording and a film all on my plate at the same time. Dad stepped in and, embarrassing though it was, wisely pulled me out of the lot and took me home to Cheshunt. For a week I did nothing and afterwards was as right as rain.

All the while, Dad was still working at Atlas Lamps. He was as independent as they come and wasn't going to give up all he'd been striving after for years to get from orange-boxes to sofas, just because his son had made it in showbiz.

Contrary to what most people imagine, the family's bank account wasn't exactly transformed overnight. Sure, I'd bought a TV set with my first cheque and a flash Sunbeam Alpine car must have looked incongruous outside a council-house. But no one suddenly came up with a cheque for a few thousand pounds. Each 'Oh Boy' appearance would have netted no more than about twenty-five pounds and it wasn't until record royalties began to filter through a year or so after I'd got going that we thought about a move. It seemed wrong to live on a council-estate if we could afford more, so we moved about six miles down the road to a semi-detached in Winchmore Hill, and filled it with brand new furniture and fitted carpets.

It was the first place we'd ever owned and the first 'improvement' we made was to virtually surround it with an enormous wooden fence to keep the fans out. Whoever lives there now still has hearts and kisses and 'I love you, Cliff' embedded in the woodwork!

Not long after Cliff and the Drifters became generally known in the pop world, someone pointed out that another group called the Drifters had been established in America for about ten years and it was unwise to duplicate the name. We'd never heard of them but when we discovered they intended releasing material in Britain we had to back out gracefully. It was Jet Harris, whom we recruited as bass player during the first tour, who suggested 'Cliff and the Shadows'. It sounded a good combination, was unanimously adopted, and went out on the next batch of records.

The Shadows of course turned out to be far more influential on the music scene than I was because they *were* the music. And that's not false modesty. Having been told to leave the guitar alone, I didn't play it again seriously until much later – not till the Shadows eventually stopped backing me. But, excluding America which has always been musically self-sufficient, the Shadows held the crown, I reckon, as the top musical group at the time.

According to a record company man in Milan, it was the Shadows' influence which sparked off the pop scene in Italy. I guess he was speaking without reference to the Beatles because obviously their contribution was immense but, in this guy's estimation at least, the Shadows were the governors!

Ironically, the original intention wasn't to launch the group as instrumentalists at all, but rather as vocalists. Before we teamed up Hank and Bruce had had a minor vocal success with Charlie Chester's son, Pete, in a group called 'The Chesternuts'. But two successive Shadows' vocal releases flopped horribly and it took singer/songwriter Jerry Lordan, who worked with us at one point, to suggest that they released one of his own instrumental compositions, 'Apaché'. They did of course and it was a million-seller. From then on, their tag was indelibly 'instrumentalists'– the first backing group to make it in their own right.

A lot of time in those days was spent touring and, even though I was lucky enough to miss out on the depressing circuit of fifth-rate clubs and seedy back-street digs, it was hard slog. I've never been a great lover of coach travel but it was a matter of 'grin, be sick, and bear it'. For two years we almost lived in a coach, haring from one theatre to the next, and after a while my system gave up the struggle and accepted it. Every tour was memorable for one reason or another but there were two which, for a naïve little lad with a pink jacket, were unique experiences.

The first was to America, where I swopped the famous jacket for a white shark-skin suit, and the other was to South Africa, where I gave a kind of Papal blessing from a hotel balcony!

America was fabulous. I was billed as 'An Added Attraction from Great Britain' in a gigantic roadshow headlining stars like Frankie Avalon, Bobby Rydell, Clyde McPhatter, the Clovers, Sammy Turner, and a whole batch of others who seemed to come and go. The package was promoted as 'The Biggest Show of Stars for 1960'. It ran for six weeks and we must have covered as much ground as a Presidential candidate. The shows were terrific and the audiences lapped up the rock 'n roll stuff. Tumultuous applause from an American audience was somehow rather special, although the nicest tribute, I think, came from our black road manager, who asked the whole coachload of artists to applaud 'our wonderful friends from Great Britain'.

Yet ironically that whistle-stop tour did nothing for me professionally. I was there for a three-week tour during the Cuba crisis and, between us, Cuba and I emptied the theatres! The problem was a total lack of liaison with the record companies. To make an impact in one town, or even a whole string of towns, is one thing; to impress the States as a whole is quite another. In America, more than anywhere else in the world, there has

A courtesy call to Laurence Harvey during his
London season in 'Camelot'.

Johannesburg's Eloff Street was closed to make way
for sightseers. That's me, somewhere on the left,
giving a kind of Papal blessing!

OPPOSITE Sharing Variety Club Awards in 1961 with
Helen Shapiro and Rita Tushingham.

to be a co-ordinating promotion machine – a record company that's committed to making an artist a major attraction and prepared to invest a colossal sum of money in promotion. That didn't happen so we missed out.

Then, two years later, we blew another opportunity when, on the strength of our film 'The Young Ones', I was asked to appear on the Ed Sullivan chat show, a programme consistently at the top of America's TV viewing ratings. I went over all ready to do 'Living Doll' and 'Move it', instead of which they gave me a straw hat and a Charlie Chaplin cane and I was told to do the music-hall sequence from 'The Young Ones' or nothing at all. Apparently no one argued with Ed Sullivan so my first major TV airing in the States was as a young vaudeville singer. It was another seventeen years before I made the effort to put them right!

South Africa was a very different kettle of fish. In America we were curiosity value, known as stars in Britain but totally unknown west of Ireland. In South Africa we had already had huge record success and arrived, for want of a better description, as 'established rock 'n roll stars'.

I've never had a reception like it anywhere in the world before or since. Johannesburg Airport was crammed. Gary Player, who I'd never met, loaned his red Continental convertible and, after shouting hellos through a microphone to thousands of cheering, waving people, we zoomed off to our hotel. What I didn't know was that the radio was blaring out exactly what time we would be passing such-and-such a corner and, as a result, our whole route was lined with kids screaming and craning their necks to get a glimpse of a bunch of bewildered boys still trying to catch their breaths after the flight and not really knowing what had hit them.

Nearer the city centre the crowds were even denser. People were hanging out of windows at the tops of buildings, and it seemed that everyone – shopkeepers and office-workers – had taken time off to be there. At the top of Eloff Street, where we were staying, there was a gigantic banner stretched across the road with 'Welcome, Cliff and the Shadows', and the whole of this famous shopping area was jam-packed with what the police reckoned to be ten or twelve thousand people. It was all too much to digest. Then the chants started: 'We want Cliff, we want Cliff.' Somehow, with the help of dozens of police, we got from the car into the hotel, the only casualty being my woollen tie, which was stretched by grabbing hands to about six feet long. Hopefully I was as near as I'll ever get to being throttled!

Then came the Pope bit. I was shoved out on to the balcony overlooking Eloff Street and a vast sea of faces. I waved and thousands and thousands of arms and handkerchiefs waved back. It's hard to describe the sensation. Every adjective, every superlative would work. It was total elation – an

'Just a little off the leg, sir?'

unbelievable, once-in-a-lifetime experience. Today one of my proudest possessions is a black-and-white movie newsreel shot at Johannesburg Airport and Eloff Street by Pathe Cinema News. Not many of my friends have seen it but just occasionally I run it through to convince myself that it really happened, and to prove to any doubting Thomases that the Beatles and the Rolling Stones didn't have a monopoly on crowds!

'The Young Ones' took my career a significant step forward. The bad boy image had already receded a little and gentler songs like 'Living Doll' and 'Travelling Light' were getting through to a much wider audience. When reviewers say that my music hasn't changed over seventeen years, I feel like blowing a loud raspberry. It changed drastically over the first two years, for a start, and, to my mind, it's changed just about every year since then. Anyway, mums and dads were beginning to appear in the audiences at concerts and the outrageous stage gear made way for a less bolshie appearance.

But it was the film that clinched it. For family appeal it was a winner, and had the distinction of being the first out-and-out musical film success produced in England by the English. Originally, no one believed it would be the box-office smash it proved to be although, after the first three or four days' rushes, the whole studio began to catch something of the potential, and what was originally a shoestring budget was suddenly injected with a further few thousands.

Oddly enough, I'd set my mind against being any kind of film celebrity. In the first film, 'Serious Charge', I certainly wasn't the star, so responsibility for bringing in the crowds wasn't mine. The fact that 'Living Doll' was a Number One hit and everyone came to see me sing it was pure accident! The intention was similarly low-key with 'Expresso Bongo' which followed. Laurence Harvey, Yolande Donlan and Sylvia Sims were the draw names and had more to lose than I if the film died. My theory was to appear in films with real acting stars, let them do all the work and attract the audiences, whilst I'd gain valuable experience and make my mark in small 'bit' parts until I felt able to cope with a lead role. Consequently, when 'The Young Ones' was offered, whilst I was naturally excited in one way, I wasn't overkeen to ruin the cunning strategy.

As I say, no one dreamed we would be responsible for the box-office draw of the year, and it was nonsense really to be voted over and above all the established movie stars who featured in films that year. But it happened and I gained a vast amount in terms of experience, insight and friendship through it. Robert Morley, who was with me in the film, for instance, was incredible. Someone had warned me that playing alongside Robert would be difficult. He didn't tolerate fools gladly and a bunch of raw beginners was likely to try his patience. That really stuck in my mind, and I was so nervous working with him that I blew a couple of lines and that meant a major retake. Before I could get a word in, Robert said, 'I'm awfully sorry, Cliff, you'll have to excuse an old dodderer like me but I've made a mistake.' I knew full well it was my fault but I felt it was tremendously kind and generous of him to take the blame. I'm sure he didn't have any respect for me as an actor because I wasn't one, but his thoughtfulness for me as a person was quite a lesson.

'The Young Ones' was shot in and around Elstree, with the exception of a kind of old music-hall sequence, which for me was the highlight and which we filmed actually on the stage at the derelict Finsbury Park Empire. We cleared the dust from the existing lights, used the tattered old curtains, packed the auditorium with people, and achieved a genuine music-hall nostalgia that would have been well-nigh impossible to re-create under studio conditions.

Weeks later the Finsbury Park Empire was demolished and, in a way, I suppose my kind of entertainment was partly responsible. The chain of old Empire Theatres was traditionally vaudeville. They had a terrific life but people were preferring pop to variety and the Empires only did good business when people like myself were there.

I thought it was a terrific compliment to be one of five or six artists asked by the Empire management to guarantee one season a year. Harry Secombe was another, I remember. If we could do it, the theatre would stay open; if not, it would be forced to close. Sadly, for my part, it was an impossible undertaking; overseas trips and an increasingly heavy schedule ruled out any kind of regular commitment.

Obviously the financial backers of 'The Young Ones' were laughing all the way to the bank and felt that such a successful formula could be squeezed a little harder. The result was 'Summer Holiday', another Cliff and the Shadows romp, with what fast became an off-camera, as well as on-camera, clique – Richard O'Sullivan, Melvin Hayes, Jeremy Bullock and Una Stubbs.

We really were just a bunch of kids enjoying a fabulous six weeks driving a London bus around Greece, and that's what comes over. All very unpretentious and as much a documentary about our own fun and relaxed relationships as an attempt at a serious storyline. The crowds in Athens Square, gaping at the bus, added another touch of reality. Normally in filming the spectators have to be kept at bay: in 'Summer Holiday' the more they stared the better. To my mind, the end result was better than 'The Young Ones' but, although it started with a budget of over half a million pounds, I don't think it achieved quite the same financial success.

OVERLEAF Robert Morley's sense of rhythm in 'The Young Ones' left a lot to be desired!

Believe it or not, I might have had Barbra Streisand playing alongside me in 'Summer Holiday' but, in our wisdom, we turned her down! Herbert Ross, who choreographed both 'The Young Ones' and 'Summer Holiday', had staged Barbra's first Broadway show and was overboard about her. Every night apparently there was fantastic audience reaction. Would you believe that when the producer flew over to see her he thought she wasn't right for the part! Maybe, for my sake, it was just as well: she would probably have stolen every review going, but imagine the billing: 'Cliff Richard and co-star Barbra Streisand'!

As they say, you can't win 'em all!

By the end of 'Summer Holiday', I was getting accustomed to the discipline of filming. On stage of course, just one good performance is all that's demanded; on a film set, that same performance has to be repeated identically again and again, perhaps a dozen times, so that close-ups can match long shots and right-side profiles marry with left-side, and so on and so on. It all demands a lot of patience and self-control, and physically it's shattering. But for me the permanency of the end project more than compensates. However brilliant a live stage performance, it's transitory. When the curtain falls, it's over for good. A brilliant film performance, on the other hand, is captured for ever, and one's appreciation of it can grow, instead of diminish, with time.

There was a third film in the same mould – 'Wonderful Life'. Forgive me if I don't dwell on it; it was a flop, a disaster from the word go. The location was the Canary Islands, noted for its exceptional sunlight and golden sands. We were there for ten weeks and it rained and the golden volcanic sands turned a murky black. On film it would have resembled a Welsh mining valley so we waited, and when eventually the rain stopped the sand took four days to dry out and regain its colour.

The whole thing was a drag and the only worthwhile sequence in the film was what was called 'The History of the Movies'. It was described on our call-sheets as 'the bad weather standby'. In fact we spent more time on that fifteen-minute section than we did on the rest put together, and it certainly shows. I believe it took six or seven years for 'Wonderful Life' to make money. It wasn't the best end to a trilogy of British musicals!

On location in the Canary Islands with Richard O'Sullivan for 'Wonderful Life'.

The moment of terror with a rubber crocodile
during 'Wonderful Life'.

The record-breaking Palladium pantomime 'Aladdin'
gave The Shadows the chance to write, as well as to
perform, a whole string of hit melodies. Left to right:
Brian Bennett, Bruce Welch, myself, Hank Marvin
and John Rostill.

6 Another Voice

AND ALL THE time that I was busy being me, God, I supposed, was equally busy being God. That is, if I supposed anything. Occasionally a press man would ask about religion and I'd say I believed in God and was Church of England. Theoretically I wasn't an atheist but in practice there wasn't much difference. The God scene wasn't relevant. It didn't interest me and I was, and still am, too mentally lazy to pay much attention to things that don't grab me from the start.

Right down the line I was Mr Average, sticking to a kind of ingrained convenient-enough moral code, but with no inclination whatever to take it further.

After all, why should I? Life was fabulous. At twenty-one, I was being paid for the only thing I ever wanted to do, the fans were screaming, and career-wise I had it made. Endless opportunities in films, television and recording were opening up. If it was lonely at the top, I couldn't imagine why; around me were people I liked, friends I worked with, and family I loved and lived with.

And then, very very faintly, something inside said, 'Please, I'm not satisfied.'

I don't know really what sparked it off, although I usually put it down to my father's death. He'd been ill for about six months and during that time our relationship changed quite drastically. A heart condition forced him, for the first time, to depend on other people.

He had to accept that his son would have to mend the fuse and cut the lawn, and there was nothing he could even contribute. He hated it, but somehow it brought us much closer together.

But, boy, was he stubborn! Doctors, he reckoned, were all quacks and didn't know what they were talking about. Smoking, he was told, was definitely dangerous and should be cut out completely, but he knew better. Even when he was in hospital in an oxygen tent he managed to unzip it from the inside and was just lighting up when a nurse spotted him.

His death, from a thrombosis, after being in hospital for two or three weeks, was a shock. I was really quite shattered and subconsciously it may have triggered off much more than I realised. All I am sure of is that about six months after he died I was working in Australia and, for the first time in my career, felt absolutely empty. Outwardly nothing had changed: audience reaction was still as fervent, friends were as friendly, but somewhere something was missing. On stage it was fine, the same total enjoyment and elation, but afterwards a kind of classic anticlimax.

It was more curiosity than desperation that prompted me to try a spirit medium. If there were any truth in the life after death business, I thought, I'd try to contact my father, who may know what was wrong. It wasn't that I wanted to re-establish any link with him for its own sake; I just wanted an academic answer to something I couldn't fathom. He had no use for life any more but I had!

Thank goodness I never got to that medium, and it was Brian Locking – Licorice, we called him – who put me off. Licorice was currently bass player in the Shadows and very casually I mentioned one evening my plan to sit in on a séance. There was instant eruption; on no account was I even to consider the idea; it was dangerous and absolutely wrong. I'd never seen Licorice so agitated or heard him so totally certain about anything before. I was quite unprepared for the flare-up and even more taken aback when Licorice pulled a Bible out of his pocket and began reading out verses of Scripture which expressly forbade any dabbling with spirits or mediums.

Now I knew Licorice had some kind of religious connection but had no idea at all that he was a convinced Jehovah's Witness. Two things impressed me: firstly, that the Bible, which I'd always thought of in terms of history and dusty irrelevance, should have anything to say about an issue which affected me personally. Admittedly it didn't give the answer I wanted but an answer it was and its direction was unquestionable. Secondly, I was impressed with Licorice's own conviction; it was so obviously important to him that I shouldn't become involved, and I warmed to that sincerity.

The outcome of what seemed a chance confrontation was that I dug out my own Bible and began going with Licorice to Jehovah's Witness meetings. So did Hank and Brian Bennett, our new drummer, who already had some nominal JW involvement.

It was good to be anonymous. One of a crowd in a Kingdom Hall congregation made a welcome change from star treatment and attention that was lavished on me elsewhere. The meetings themselves were enlightening. Speakers had the same ring of authority as Licorice and what they said seemed logical and in line with Scripture. Above all, everyone was so incredibly zealous. I lapped it up with enthusiasm and virtually no discernment.

From then on, dressing-room discussion took on a very different complexion. Whenever there was opportunity, the two Brians, Hank and I would get together to study some passage of the Bible together, and the more I read the more impressed I was to see Scripture relating to modern people and current situations. During a long summer season in Blackpool, we even had a formal course of Biblical studies. One of the local JW elders came to our house every other day to give us what I thought at the time were brilliant Bible expositions. With hindsight, I realise now they were little more than recitations of official 'party line'.

Although we made no attempt to cover up our JW interest, not many people were aware of it. The family, of course, was an exception. When I arrived home from America, I was so bubbling over with the JW scene that Mum and my sisters had no way of escape. Within a day or two I'd invited a local JW to our home and after that all of us were caught up.

I remember one of my first revelations was to discover that God's name was Jehovah and that we could think of Him as a personality rather than as an abstract title. Much later I heard Shelley Burman, a Jewish comedian, put it beautifully: 'Jehovah is His name, God is His occupation!'

So at home and at work JW teaching was influencing attitudes and priorities. There was just one all-crucial reservation – commitment. Whilst I believed it, discussed it, read up all the literature, and argued and defended it, I couldn't bring myself to the crunch of public JW baptism, and that was what mattered. That was the dividing-line between being 'in' or 'out'. For over two years, I resisted all the pressure of JW acquaintances to submit to baptism. When the press quizzed me, I denied point-blank any intention. The thought of press coverage, public reaction and the possible risk to my career was terrifying. Today I can see there was more to it than that, for when I became a Christian a while later commitment versus career was never an issue.

Looking back, I believe that my whole JW involvement progressed only on one level – that of the mind. It was a kind of arid mental exercise in which I was led by various subtle means to exactly the same conclusions as all the others. There was no spiritual encounter, no personal experience of a forgiving and a loving Christ, no understanding of prayer. I wasn't even being taught Scripture, as I honestly believed at the time, but rather JW interpretation of Scripture.

There's that key statement, for example, by Jesus in John's Gospel: 'Before Abraham was, I am.' Because Jesus adopts the very term which is applied to Jehovah God in the Old Testament, the implication of divinity is crystal-clear, but JWs of course deny the divinity of Christ and so maintain that the 'I am' in all orthodox translations of the Bible is grammatically

OVERLEAF These mentally-handicapped youngsters
made an affectionate audience.

inaccurate. In their own *Watchtower* translation, they consequently change Jesus' words to: 'Before Abraham came into existence, I have been'! It sounds better, admittedly, but sadly they've rubbed out the theology. What was intended as a theological declaration has been invalidated on the grounds of better grammar!

However, none of all that dawned on me till very much later and, with some of my father's stubbornness – I was going to say pigheadedness – I refused to admit to doubts. That, to my mind, was weakness and I don't think I was a secure enough person to confess to any chinks in my armour.

Religious discussions with people outside the JW camp invariably led to argument and one member of our office staff predicted a split in the team if religion got too firm a grip. Secretly, I was uneasy. I thought a Jewish opinion might help; if the Jews were God's chosen people, I reasoned, they ought to have some answers. All I was after was a shoring-up of my own position. I came away realising that if Judaism was still looking for its Messiah, they would be hard put to identify him. Old Testament prophecy specified that he must be a direct descendant of David; with the line long since lost, the condition becomes meaningless. At least my short excursion into Judaism reassured me that in Jesus I was on the right track.

Then in July 1965 I took part in a car rally and a friendship struck there led to almost total reorientation spiritually and socially. Jay Norris, you remember, was my English teacher and ever since leaving school we'd kept in touch. Each year Jay celebrated her birthday with a car rally and I was invited.

At home, sister Joan was excited as, at fourteen, she was all starry-eyed over her class teacher, Mr Latham, and she couldn't wait for me to meet him. The idea appealed for, since Dad's death, I'd assumed some responsibility for my kid sister, and a social evening chatting about her school prospects seemed a proper paternal duty. Little did I know that Jay was busy scheming on quite another level. A nominal Roman Catholic, she was very anti my JW interests; instinctively she felt I was being led astray and wanted someone to 'put me right'. She too had a high regard for Bill Latham, who was head of religious education at school, and thought he might have the answers to some of my entrenched JW opinions.

So it was that I found myself a passenger in – surprise, surprise – Bill Latham's car. Well, we came runners-up in the rally, had a useful chat about Joan, got on quite easily but, much to Jay's disappointment, didn't get round to religion at all. But Mrs Norris is a determined lady and a few months later saw Bill, Jay, and another school colleague, Graham Disbrey, invited to our relatively new home in Nazeing.

The semi-detached in Winchmore Hill had served well, but the more

OVERLEAF, ABOVE Some of the regular 'holiday gang' with newly-discovered friends off the island of Madeira.

BELOW All at sea off Madeira!

established I became as a pop artist, the greater was the need for privacy and somewhere to entertain. Rookswood, in those two respects, was ideal. It was tucked away in eleven acres in the Essex countryside, although still no more than ten miles from Cheshunt. It was a beautiful house, with original panelling in the dining room from Hampton Court; there was a billiards room, six bedrooms, four enormous reception rooms, and the most fabulous gardens. There was even a staff cottage, complete with gardener and wife. Thirty-two thousand pounds was the price we paid for it; two years later we sold it at a £6,000 profit, and I've never lived in such a stately place since.

Anyway, back to our get-together, and this time Jay had made sure that the agenda was understood – religion. It wasn't really as sober or as sticky as it sounds. All of us had opinions and we were all keen to express them. Inevitably there were brick walls – huge, impenetrable ones, it seemed to me then. I guess I'd picked up a typical JW 'tunnel vision' attitude towards many basic Christian doctrines and nothing that Bill or Graham said shed much light.

In fairness, of course, I had no intention of shifting my ground. As far as I was concerned, I was right and they were wrong. That old fundamental chestnut, the Trinity, was a major battleground, and I still believe that most regular Christians haven't really thought through their own beliefs on this one and are content to trot out the 'one in three and three in one' formula, as though that tidily explained the whole thing. It was this non-clarity that I felt was wrong about regular Christianity.

Today I've grasped the 'one in three' business but it needs, I'm sure, to be surrounded by so much more explanation and qualification than we usually give it. To say Jesus is God and leave it as a bald statement is misleading; when Jesus was on earth the heavens were not evacuated; God was still there and Jesus prayed to Him. Today I still meet Christians, clergy included, who say things that I desperately want them to qualify. When they don't, I just wonder if they really understand what they're saying.

So there were these two young Christian teachers, trying to explain to me how you could possibly have one God and yet three Gods. And their point-scoring was zero. When they left, nothing was resolved. Jay was just as concerned. What she didn't know and I didn't admit was that something had got through. Not words or arguments, but two people who bothered me because of an assurance about Jesus that I didn't have and, what's more, I'd never recognised in other JWs.

I'd have let it go, I think, if Bill hadn't invited me to a further chat session, this time at his house in Finchley. For this occasion, Bill had recruited reinforcements in the very able person of David Winter, who was then editor of a Christian magazine and who subsequently joined the BBC as producer of religious programmes. David is an exceptional communicator and spelt out points of doctrine and the fundamentals of the Christian faith clearly and logically. It made more sense, but I was still unconvinced. Again, though, there was the same awareness of something different and appealing about these men. They talked about Jesus as though they knew Him. Gently, and at first imperceptibly, my JW platform began to rock.

Then came a shrewd move on Bill's part. Would I sit in on a Sunday afternoon Crusader class? It was shrewd because, had it been an invitation to church, I'd have turned it down flat. Church, according to JWs, is of the devil and so are all who sail in her. But Crusaders wasn't church – just a group of youngsters who met in a relaxed club kind of atmosphere to be taught about the Christian life. Being part of that presented no threat and, as far as I could see, no compromise.

That first Sunday was an odd experience for everyone. There was I, trying to look as nonchalant as possible, in the back row of a classroom with thirty or so goggling schoolboys in front of me in various stages of incredulity, embarrassment and excitement. It was a weird situation. They didn't know why I was there and, in all honesty, I wasn't too sure myself. If the showbiz crowd could have seen me, they'd have thought I was crazy.

But the Crusader kids were terrific and it took no time for the ice to break and any pedestals to be smashed. After three or four Sundays, I was accepted as part of the class and, in case I still needed to prove I was human, a few days on a cruiser on the Norfolk Broads later that year did the trick. When you've been rugby-tackled, flung to the ground and sat on by a bunch of beefy fourteen-year-olds, there's little point in standing on your dignity.

That journey to the Broads was a driver's nightmare. I had a big black Cadillac at the time and there were about half-a-dozen kids packed in the front and back. With its hundred-and-one gadgets, the sleek automobile provided a kind of three-hour novelty ride and the electric windows, up and down like yo-yos, were never quite the same afterwards.

As the months went on, more and more of the Crusader brand of evangelical Christian teaching was edging under my skin. One misconception that had to go very early on was that 'orthodox' Christians, apart naturally from JWs, were hopelessly divided. At Crusaders it just wasn't so: Bill was an Anglican, Graham a Baptist, and another leader was an elder in a Brethren assembly. Yet in their teaching and in their priorities, there was nothing to tell them apart. There was no question of division. It was the same Jesus they professed to know and who, they said, was available to me too.

For a year I went on with the Jekyll and Hyde kind of spiritual existence – one foot dangling with decreasing confidence in the JW camp, another stepping tentatively into a whole new fabulous Christian scene, which was a million miles removed from the traditional lifeless church experience I remembered as a child.

What happened during that amazing year was a slow process of me waking up to the fact that Bill and others were talking about something quite different from my JW experiences. Mine was a theory that I could argue and defend; theirs were words wrapped round a Person whom I didn't know.

The crunch came at a Whitsun camp in Lewes and, for the umpteenth time, I was doing verbal battle with Bill over some issue that had cropped up in one of his talks. By then we'd become very good friends but on this occasion I felt really annoyed by one of his questions: *'How do you know you're a Christian?'*

It was a fair, relevant and necessary question and, with hindsight, I'm thankful he asked it. Faced with the same question before, I'd always waffled out an answer but at that Whit camp my hackles went up because for the first time it dawned on me that I couldn't honestly answer it. I knew Bill could; he would talk about a personal relationship with Christ and a day when, as a schoolboy, he consciously committed his life to Christ. But for me there was no relationship, no assurance – just a package of second-hand dogmas.

A few weeks after that camp I became a Christian. Appropriately enough, it was at Bill's house in Finchley. I was staying there throughout the filming of 'Finders Keepers' at Pinewood Studios, and one evening I read the words of Jesus in the book of Revelation: 'Behold, I stand at the door and knock; whoever hears my voice and opens the door, I will come in.' The only way I can explain it is that that must have been God's moment for me, because, although I'd been through it all in my mind many times before, I only realised then that a relationship was a two-way thing and I'd contributed nothing.

So, in that front bedroom in Finchley, I lay on the bed and mouthed a very hesitant prayer. It was something like: 'All right, Jesus, I'm aware that you're knocking – you'd better come in and take over.' It was nothing more complicated than that. No flashes of light, no voices in the ear, no sudden visions. All I recall is that I meant what I said and was willing for the consequences.

People often knock or try to explain away Christian conversions as emotional illusions which wear off. Now I happen to be pretty familiar with my emotions. Like a lot of stage people, I'm what you'd call an emotional kind of person. At a weepy film I'll be through my third tissue

OVERLEAF 'Summer Holiday's' famous red bus amid film crew and Greek countryside.

62.6

before most of the audience have finished their choc-ice. If anyone's vulnerable to emotional pressure, it's me.

That's why I know what I'm talking about when I say that what happened that evening was nothing to do with emotional jiggery-pokery. It was a decision not prompted by a temporary mood or a hellfire sermon, but by a cool and reasoned-out conclusion – arrived at after months of hassle – that I needed Jesus.

In the re-telling a hint of drama would have helped – but it's easy to embroider for effect, and in truth there was none. Even next day I didn't leap off to Pinewood consciously thinking, 'Today's my first day as a Christian.'

Yet, without the faintest shadow of a doubt, that sober and almost anticlimactic evening in suburban London marked the turning-point of my life. Today – eleven years on – there's the overwhelming evidence that Jesus accepted the invitation – eleven fabulous years of getting to know Him.

7 My Little Isaac

ST PAUL SPENT two years after his conversion sorting himself out in Tarsus. I did much the same in Finchley. A few months before I'd only heard of the place as a gag on a Goon LP. Suddenly it became the focal point for new relationships and for what was, in effect, a radical change of lifestyle.

What I needed more than anything else after that initial commitment was the encouragement of patient and understanding Christians; an occasional meeting every now and again wasn't enough. I wanted to soak in a Christian environment where I could learn and grow up. As usual God's timing was perfect.

My family at Nazeing were beginning to go their separate ways. Donna had already married, Jackie was on the verge of it, and I knew my mother was planning to marry a friend of the family, Derek Bodkin, whom I now call 'Pop'! Whether I liked it or not, the family was breaking up and I hadn't the slightest inclination to stay on in splendid isolation at Rookswood. Already I had stayed for a while with Bill and Mrs Latham, and when they mentioned their intention of moving it seemed the most logical thing to join forces. All three of us got on tremendously well and Mamie adapted easily and generously to a second son, despite his peculiar hours. In fact we didn't move far – only a couple of miles, from Finchley to a nice Georgian-type house in Totteridge. It wasn't as grand as Rookswood, but a good deal more cosy!

Now don't get the idea that showbiz was suddenly phased out. A panto season at the Palladium, recording sessions, TV and concert tours at home and overseas kept the career going in top gear. But now my attitude to it was different. It hadn't ceased to be important but it was no longer *all*-important. Show-business had its place, but so had Crusaders, Bible study nights, Broads cruises and summer camps. I guess it must have seemed crazy to the showbiz crowd. 'What have you got planned for the weekend?' they would ask. The answer usually produced a flicker of astonishment and a prompt change of subject.

One of my earliest Christian-type decisions was to ensure that, whenever possible, Sundays were kept free from professional bookings. It wasn't a negative rule – I just wanted that day to do other things. As in everything else, my management were fabulous and ever since have co-operated right down the line.

Funnily enough, it took quite a while before I felt sufficiently sure or confident to get involved in any church activity. Obviously my JW thinking wasn't wiped out overnight and even now I still have a few ingrained attitudes left over from those days of highly efficient indoctrination.

Church really was a very major problem at the start. For years I'd been led to believe that the whole established structure was of the devil and I must confess that my recollections of the lifeless ritual in Cheshunt and India didn't help. Gradually and tactfully Bill eased me into attending his own Anglican church, St Paul's, Finchley, where he was a lay-reader. But, boy, was I suspicious at first! Throughout every sermon I'd be on edge, waiting for the vicar to pronounce some wild heresy! The Trinity probably bugged me more than anything and I used to get really worked up at the clichéd jargon that Christians trotted out so glibly. Maybe it was ultra-presumptuous but I often had a shrewd suspicion that they didn't really know what they meant and I wanted desperately some kind of qualification or explanation.

Anyway, it didn't take me long to realise that the Church was bigger than the building or its services and that, as a Christian, I was automatically part of it. I was confirmed by the Bishop of London within a year, and on Christmas Eve, 1966, I took my first communion. I remember coming home just in time for the midnight service, after doing two shows at the Palladium. It was a marvellous spiritual and emotional experience – the first time I'd taken bread and wine, and my first Christmas as a Christian. Both would be taboo in JW circles for, to their way of thinking, communion is a privilege confined to the chosen 144,000, and Christmas remains a pagan festival with no relevance for Christians.

Meanwhile, Crusader activities were grabbing more and more of my time, and Sunday afternoon class provided an ideal training-ground for communicating what I'd found. I must have been pretty awful at leading choruses and giving talks, but I did my bit and learned to smile when the kids told me what they thought of my latest single. I reckon I learned much more than they did and, I tell you, those talks were more nerve-shattering than any stage appearance.

I'm not sure whether my eventual election to full leadership was really warranted; certainly I put in nothing like the hours that other leaders contributed, and I don't know what I was able to achieve in terms of leadership. But it was a responsibility and an expression of confidence which I appreciated and took seriously. Maybe there was some value to the kids in meeting someone from the pop scene to whom Christ was all-important and totally relevant, and who was simply there and available to take them round the zoo or the Bus Museum or skipper a cruiser on the Norfolk Broads for a week at Easter.

The younger boys especially revelled in the autograph routine and loved a kind of 'Protect Cliff from the public' role. One enterprising bunch at a Crusader camp on Herm in the Channel Islands adopted an 'If you can't beat them, fleece them' policy, and every time I was approached for an autograph one of the boys would appear from nowhere with a plastic cup and insist on a donation to a children's home which had a camp in an adjacent field. People coughed up very graciously and at the end of the holiday I think we handed well over £50 to the superintendent.

Probably it was through some Crusader activity that other Christian groups around the country got wind of 'Cliff's conversion'. There had been a few guarded Christian newspaper articles which hinted at some spiritual experience, and that signalled the beginning of a whole new category of correspondence – the 'Would Cliff be free to take part in . . . ?' type of letter. At first it was a trickle and probably it would have stayed that way for years had it not been for Billy Graham.

Many people seem to think that Billy had a hand in my conversion. He hadn't and I'd never heard him speak till the Earl's Court crusade of 1966. Somehow the Graham organisation must have been told of my conversion and one morning the invitation came. Would I speak about my faith during the crusade's ' Youth Night'?

In retrospect, I think that invitation crystallised many things. I was never in any doubt about accepting but knew full well that, in terms of a public stand, this was the crunch. Twenty-five thousand people attended the Graham rallies and world press coverage was a certainty. The media would have a field day and the headlines were predictable: 'Cliff gets religion', 'Cliff and Billy Graham' . . . ' You'll have to be prepared to lose a lot of fans,' said someone. The whole thing would be slanted, misrepresented and misunderstood.

Suddenly I was aware that I'd no qualifications and no experience in anything other than singing. If the career collapsed, I was patently useless at anything else.

Today, with more than eleven years of Christian experience behind me, I've learned that the more we depend on God the more dependable we find He is. If my career had ended then, or indeed if it ends tomorrow, I'm absolutely confident that He would lead me on somewhere else.

But really there was no battle, even then. I'm a person who tends to see issues as either black or white. Sometimes, I admit, that's not good. In this instance I know it was – I was either a Christian or not. If I was and if God was for real, then there was no dilemma. It either meant everything or nothing.

It took me ten minutes to say my piece and sing a song on that Earl's Court platform and that ten minutes is photographed in my memory in every stark detail. Even thinking about it now brings me out in a cold sweat.

I'm not a very good guitarist today but then I was even worse. I knew there was no chance of being sufficiently 'together' and co-ordinated to accompany myself, so Tedd Smith, Billy Graham's regular pianist, agreed to back me for 'It is no secret'. Having got to the podium, I gripped Billy's desk, just in case the legs didn't hold out, sang the song and said what I had to say. The problem came when I'd finished. Somehow my arms had locked in a kind of extended gripping position and, half-blinded from hundreds of flashlights, I must for all the world have looked like Frankenstein's monster lurching back to my seat. I know odd things happen to the body when you're scared or nervous but I've never experienced anything like it before or since.

I should explain an added complication which didn't exactly ease the tension. The whole episode was being filmed for the Billy Graham production 'Two a Penny' which I'd also agreed to appear in. Now the main shooting of that film wasn't scheduled till several months later, but it was known that one scene would require my character's involvement in an authentic crusade situation.

Jamie Hopkins, this rather snide character in the film, was supposed to have wheedled his way on to the Graham platform and was to appear cynical and critical of the whole set-up. I remember sitting there with a bunch of cards in my top pocket and on each card was an instruction from director, Jim Collier. When I removed a card, the camera-man, who was hiding, supposedly discreetly, among the potted plants at the front of the platform, knew I was about to switch on the acting.

Each card had something like 'Look towards Billy and sneer', 'Think that the audience must be a bunch of sheep to take it all in'. Somehow I got through it all, and even the acting couldn't have been that bad for I received at least one furious 'and you call yourself a Christian' type of letter about my 'appalling behaviour' during Billy's address.

One of the people who encouraged me most around this time was my manager, Peter Gormley. Now Peter wouldn't claim to have any specifically Christian commitment but his backing and understanding of my position have been something exceptional.

Peter is unique among theatrical managers, for his major concern is for the happiness and fulfilment of his artists, not only in their careers but in their personal lives and, believe me, that's a rare kind of priority in our profession. Peter was convinced that my participation in the Graham crusade was right and when, soon after that, I plucked up courage to tell him I was considering leaving show-business, his reaction was predictably consistent: if that was what I wanted, he advised, then that's what I should do. If I held out and went on with something I didn't have my heart in, then I'd do a bad job.

It was wise advice, but, as you know, things didn't turn out that way.

This was my second 'post-conversion' crisis point and came about, I suppose, through my own immaturity as a Christian. While my Christian friends outside show-business were engaged in what, to my mind, were far more obviously 'Christian jobs', I felt frustrated that, after just a year, I'd achieved about all that was possible for Christ in the entertainment world. I'd already made my statement to those who wanted to hear, the media had done their stuff and, after the crusade in particular, had written endless stories about 'the new Cliff Richard', but all the journalists' questions were the same and I found myself going over the familiar testimony again and again. What else was there to say? Ahead there could only be a dead end. The reporters would have exhausted the new angle and then what?

Maybe there was an element of guilt too somewhere about earning much more than my Christian friends who were doing mundane jobs, and I don't doubt that subconsciously I was already being influenced by the evangelical suspicion of art generally and theatre in particular. Could a Christian really stay in entertainment without compromising his faith?

The obvious alternative was teaching. Bill and Graham were doing a good job at Cheshunt and I appreciated the potential influence of Christian teachers. Besides, teaching itself I considered an art form, and part and parcel of the communications business. Crusaders had shown me I could cope with a classroom of kids!

A visit to a teachers' training college in Hertfordshire confirmed that there would be every chance of a place in the following year's intake, even though I didn't have the regulation GCE subjects.

'A real desire to teach is the important thing,' I remember the principal saying. 'Most students who come here don't have it!' Even so, I had no faith at all in my own academic ability so decided to see how I fared at one O-level in RE.

With some guidance from Bill, I wrote reams of notes, laboured through a dozen or more essays, hated the personal discipline involved, and eventually sat the exam in a large cupboard at a grammar school in Sussex. Every so often a teacher poked his head round the door to make sure I wasn't cheating. I wasn't and I passed!

They wanted elegance and good looks for the
parts in 'Take Me High'. Tony Andrews
and I got the job!

Lovely Ann Holloway was my leading lady in 'Two a
Penny'. She became familiar to British tv viewers in
'Father, dear Father'.

OPPOSITE Not quite high enough to make 'Congratulations' the
Eurovision winner at the Royal Albert Hall!

Meanwhile, the countdown was under way. The fan-club, about 40,000 strong at that point, was phased out; petitions began to arrive, insisting that I change my mind; and an historic press conference was called to make it all official. Maybe it was our fault for not spelling things out clearly enough but subsequent reports mentioned a bizarre selection of spiritual callings, from a monk to a missionary. Nevertheless, all agreed on the essence: Cliff Richard was quitting show-business.

The subsequent about-turn was all very embarrassing and I can hardly blame a few pressmen for reading in ulterior motives. In fact it took a flurry of open doors and the counsel of one man to help me see that I was on the wrong route. The doors led to the production of a gospel album, 'Good News', to a series of religious television shows, numerous chat shows on both radio and television, and to 'Two a Penny'. And the point was, I initiated none of them.

Here was the career which I'd written off as useless to God, throwing up positive and unique opportunities to communicate Christ. I had a ready-made listening audience yet I was actively trying to be rid of them. It was Jim Collier, a man I think the world of, who put the situation sharply and finally into focus. 'Why, when people get converted,' he said, 'do they want to leave their jobs and do something else? Our role is to be Christians first and foremost where we are.'

I suppose, if I'd been a lot less hasty and prayed about the thing more seriously, I'd have never taken things so far. It just never struck me that God may have had a hand in my past as well as my present and future, and that this was the career He intended.

Fortunately, no real damage was done and, as I'm convinced that everything we've experienced in the past makes us what we are today, I guess it was a useful part of the moulding process. It wasn't until Abraham was on the point of sacrificing Isaac that God made it clear he could keep him. It may sound over-dramatic but, for me, that situation represented my little Isaac. When I was prepared to give the career up, God said, 'Don't, we'll use it.'

A few years later, I remember reliving much of the tension, this time on behalf of that brilliant actor, James Fox. Of course God deals with people in different ways but I must confess it was a real disappointment to me when James went through with his decision to abandon acting after his conversion. James was among an acting élite and other professionals, I know, rated him very highly indeed. The arts world desperately needed a gifted Christian actor; God called out such an actor and the actor gave it up. That's not meant as a personal criticism; James was right and discerning,

I'm sure, but I can't help imagining the impact he might have made as a Christian where he was.

There was a strange irony in my being asked to play that lead role in 'Two a Penny'. For some time I'd had a growing inclination to tackle a straight dramatic role but no casting director was prepared to take me seriously as an actor. Cliff Richard was a singer who drove red buses around Athens and, try as we might, we couldn't convince anyone otherwise. As I say, it was a strange twist of fate that it was as a Christian I got an invitation to play a part that was different.

Worldwide Films, the Billy Graham film company, wanted an English actor who was a Christian and who had film experience. I guess I was the only one around who filled the categories. To my mind, it's far and away the best film I've done and it was a shame it never got a general release. The critics didn't exactly go overboard: secular press thought it was too Christian, and Christian press thought it was too secular. But what's important is that, through its story and its message, people have encountered Christ.

One of the early feedback reports was of a girl from the provinces who absconded with £200 of her firm's money. She came to London and saw the film; apparently she was so moved by it that she went straight to the Billy Graham office in Camden Town, told them what she'd done, and asked for help. The whole thing was cleared up in the courts and I gather the girl subsequently joined the fellowship of a church.

The film is still being shown in church halls and meeting-places around the country and it's been dubbed in several other languages. Goodness knows how many letters I've had from people expressing their appreciation.

Even while we shot the film, mainly on location in London, there were special things happening. For a start, Jim Collier and I spent hours talking about Jesus to Dora Bryan, who played my mum in the story. Dora was full of questions – the whys and wherefores of her own faith, and the meaning of this or that reference which she thumbed up in her Bible. The great thing was that she genuinely wanted answers and it was fabulous to be in at the beginning of her relationship with Christ.

It was Jim who set the tone of the whole film project. At first, the crew didn't know what they'd got involved in; a few days later they stopped their swearing, not because they felt obliged to but out of sheer respect for Jim; by the end, they really loved him and presented him with a silver salver inscribed 'To Gentleman Jim'.

Film crews are notoriously union-minded and sticklers for every letter of the rule-book. When we had to hurry one scene on Barnes towpath, the rushes were predictably poor. Instead of making do, every member of the team – camera crew and lighting men included – wanted to do it again. There was no fuss about overtime: they just wanted it right for Jim. That kind of co-operation is refreshing and only happens in a rare kind of working relationship.

If you get the impression I'm a Jim Collier fan, you're dead right. For a start, he's the only director I've ever worked with who actually directed me or got me to think in depth about my character. Before we went near a camera, we'd probed into the mind and motivation of every character who had anything to do with the context, and I'd written at length where I thought the emotional peaks were to come in my performance.

I'd never been so businesslike about a part before and, although the concentration gave me headaches, I felt more involved in and committed to that film than to any I'd done in the past.

Jim once said that his major talent was that he could make people act. I'd be more precise over one word. Jim can *inspire* people to act. He inspires with an energy and a sincerity which capture everyone working with him, not just principals but extras, scene-shifters – everyone.

Three years later I worked with Jim again, this time on 'His Land', a documentary type of picture which portrayed modern-day Israel in the light of prophecy from yesterday. It was a double bonus for me for, apart from Jim, there was the excitement of going to Israel as a Christian. I'd been before but it hadn't meant much. Now everything I'd read in the Bible seemed to gain a new dimension. I remember running around the Pool of Bethesda like a tourist twit, really ecstatic that I was actually at the very spot where Jesus had performed a miracle.

Through 'His Land' and 'Two a Penny' and subsequent appearances on various Billy Graham crusade platforms, my respect and admiration for Billy, both as a preacher and as a person, have grown immensely. I've never met anyone who has such a complete and composed authority. It's apparent in his public speaking and it's there too in his private conversation: authority born out of absolute conviction. In a sense, I suppose that's naturally a bit intimidating and in his company I find myself conscious of his importance. But that's my fault; in no sense is Billy intimidating as a person – his manner is warm and easy and he's more interested in listening than speaking. He has an amazing capacity to remember people's names and situations and does so not from any sort of contrived professionalism but from genuine personal interest. When you remember that Billy's parish is virtually worldwide, that's an extraordinary ability. As you'll gather, Billy rates highly in my category of 'greats' and I'm not easily bowled over by big names!

Meanwhile, a good chunk of the Christian family was busy discussing whether a pop singer who recorded love-songs and danced on television could have any kind of experience of God.

Some were adamant, and still are, that the wicked world of show-business and the Christian faith are totally incompatible. How could anyone call himself a Christian and cavort about a stage with sequinned, leggy ladies ooh-aahing in the background? Clearly, for many, it was a major problem and I understand it a little. What I didn't bargain for was a new spate of letters, allegedly from Christians, which expressed sentiments not far short of hatred.

Certainly many were spiteful and lacked any semblance of constructive concern. I remember particularly a Roman orgy sketch that I did in a television show. I was supposed to be a Christian slave given the choice of joining the orgy or being thrown to the lions. In fact I chose the lions – but you should have read the letters afterwards! I don't think I slept for a week after that for, although I'd got accustomed to the usual kind of cranky and twisted letters that everyone in public life receives, tears up and forgets, these were upsetting because they came from people with whom I believed I should be at one.

Believe it or not, we also got some flak for one half-hearted attempt to make Jamie Hopkins use true-to-life vocabulary in 'Two a Penny'. Despite Jim Collier's integrity, if we'd been absolutely honest, Jamie would have been a much worse character than he was portrayed. All the way through, we were conscious of not using certain language because, as someone put it, little old ladies from Pasadena were indirectly paying for the film through their support of the Graham organisation and they mustn't be offended!

I had to do two versions of one particular scene, I remember – one with 'damn', the other without 'damn'. How daft can you get? My sordid little character would have said something much more earthy!

If I'd been on my own, out on a limb, at the time, I think I'd have been shattered by the venom, even though for every one of the nasties there were at least a dozen really loving warm-hearted letters welcoming me into the Family. As it happened, God had seen to things and provided all that I needed to cope. A bunch of Christian friends, a suburban Anglican church, the Crusader class, and a diary!

Feeding time at home. Left to right: Kelly, Bill,
me (thinly disguised) and Mrs Latham –
Mamie to friends.

Photographs of my manager, Peter
Gormley, are hard to come by. He
slipped up during a stroll through a
Japanese market and let a camera-man
catch one shot for the record.

A lot of patience was involved before
Donna and her husband, Tim, were
able to adopt little Tay from Vietnam.

8 A Second Diary

ONE RESULT OF nearly twenty years in show-business is that I'm spoilt silly. Someone else has seen that the 'plane ticket is booked, that the hotel is fixed, that letters are answered, that I'm in the right place at the right time, that bills are paid, and that the car's got petrol.

As a result, I'm still sane, more or less, despite an enormous work-load and, in addition, I must be the world's worst admin man. Left to my own devices, I suppose I might cope eventually if I had to, but the thought appals me. For a start, I'd have to work up enthusiasm to actually open my mail, let alone reply to it, and, as my memory went prematurely senile by about fifty years, I couldn't guarantee to remember engagements. Or, if I did, the chances are I'd misread the instructions and go to the wrong place on the wrong day! I've tried keeping a diary but that didn't work and, although there's a Memory Board hanging in my loo, I forget to write anything on it!

What it amounts to, I confess, is no discipline. I need organised people around, just to ensure that I do what I ought to do, read what I ought to read, and every now and again point me in the right direction!

Now when I became a Christian that flaw could have presented a major headache. I could hardly expect Peter Gormley, David Bryce, my touring manager, or any of the girls in the office, to decide Christian priorities or to spend their free time liaising with clergy. But again there was no problem.

By this time Bill had automatically become my Christian reference point, so to speak, and undertook the onerous business of replying to the dozens of enquiries and invitations which began to arrive at home and at the office with every post. I remember him arriving back from a day's teaching and disappearing for two or three hours to bash out the replies. Later, when Bill was appointed Deputy Director of Tear Fund, he was able to offload a good deal of the secretarial work but carried on as my 'Christian Activities Organiser' – a ghastly title but we couldn't think of anything more descriptive.

Bill was, and still is, a key person in the Christian work I do. At the beginning he wisely kept me away from tackling things I wasn't ready for, and I've been more than happy to leave most of the basic decision-making as to what I should or shouldn't do to him. Right from the start, there needed to be really tight liaison between Bill and my professional office concerning schedules and all credit to both sides that there have been few, if any, clashes.

At first the meetings I did were simple affairs which amounted to singing two or three gospel songs and giving my testimony. Mostly it was at church services and Crusader classes around the country. But gradually the opportunities broadened and I found myself in university halls, cathedrals and drawing rooms, talking about the Person who had suddenly come to mean so much to me.

Let me give one piece of advice to any Christian, young or old, who might be reading this and who feels he or she hasn't progressed much in the Christian life. Get up and do something! Get involved in your local church or fellowship and be prepared to take on responsibility. I suppose I must have spoken to hundreds of thousands of Christians in the last ten years or so, but sadly many of them are the 'armchair' variety – pew-fillers who are in their element attending meetings, but are nowhere to be seen when it comes to taking on Christian leadership or responsibility.

It's only when you're involved and needing consciously to depend on God that your faith has a chance to grow. I remember hearing someone say that if you never used a limb for a long period of time, it would eventually become paralysed'– the muscles would just stop functioning. Faith is the same. If it's never exercised or exerted, it collapses. Sermon over!

For me there was plenty of exertion. Slowly, as my confidence grew, and I came to understand more fully what I was talking about, Bill and I did a kind of face-to-face, question-and-answer routine, which at a later stage still we threw open to the audience. It's in this dialogue format that I'm in my element, I suppose.

Crusaders had taught me I was no preacher. To have to mug up on a certain subject and speak from prepared notes was, for me, stifling and artificial and I did it badly. I know I often surprise interviewers, whether it be press, radio, or television, who want to tell me beforehand what they're going to ask. I far prefer not to know. The result, as far as I'm concerned anyway, is more honest and less contrived. The same goes for any Christian meeting I take part in. If my role has to be prepared or rehearsed, I fumble about and hate every minute of it. If I can be free, I might waffle but at least what I say is me; it's what I feel and what I understand. And if someone fires a question that I can't answer, then I have no qualms in saying, 'I don't know'. The onus is on me then to make sure I find out or think the issue through so I can do better next time.

More often than not, those dialogue sessions – and I've done hundreds

In Sudan and Bangladesh with Tear Fund.
OVERLEAF Playing; drinking.

of them, all over the place – have helped me more than the audience. There's nothing better than to be put on the spot and be forced to frame an opinion. And if you think that sounds mighty difficult, remember that it's not my authority but Scripture's that I try to apply, and that there's a promise that God will give us the words to say in that kind of critical situation.

I'm convinced that that promise still stands and I've proved it over and over again. You'd be surprised to find how the same old questions crop up, whether you're at a secondary school or a post-graduate conference. The vocabulary is different but that's all. To my mind though, the very fact that the questions are asked is a healthy sign. I know some local organisers are doubtful whether anyone will open their mouth in a crowded hall or church, but I've yet to find a group who've been that shy.

Even more encouraging to me is the spirit behind the questioning. Early on it was often cynical and aimed at catching me out. Today that's rare. Sure, there's plenty of shallow curiosity around but, for the most part, people ask because they want to know.

It was David Winter's idea that I should deal with some of the most frequently asked questions in a book. David, now a producer in the BBC's Religious Broadcasting Department, was another Christian friend whom I'd come to value. Like Bill, he was a lay-reader at St Paul's and a gifted communicator. Prior to my conversion, he was the first person I'd met who could explain doctrines such as the Trinity and the divinity of Christ in terms I could understand, and two or three years afterwards I remember calling on him to spell it out explicitly again when a couple of Jehovah's Witnesses came for a 'reclaim' attempt in the dressing room of the London Palladium.

One of them was the old Shadows' guitarist, Brian Locking, who by that time was more or less in full-time JW work. I knew it was a 'let's get Cliff back on the rails' session and, remembering their two-to-one technique, I wanted David on hand to keep the balance.

It was a sad interview really because it was so obvious that, as individuals, they were missing out on the very heart of the gospel. One question that David put to Brian crystallised it: 'Do you really know you have salvation?' And Brian didn't. He hoped that, when the world ended, he would be acceptable in God's sight but that's as far as he could go. Jesus' death provided the possibility of salvation but, in the final analysis, it was dependent on his own obedience. As far as I know, Brian is still an active JW, and who am I to say we won't be reunited in heaven, but as a reclaim effort it failed miserably and only underlined my relief that I'd not become more embroiled.

Encounters in Bangladesh.

Anyway, David's idea for the book was that I should simply talk answers to a few questions into a tape-recorder and he would do the rest. It was so painless and I feel guilty that the book should have come out at all under my name alone. But it did and *The Way I See It,* together with its successors, *Questions* and *The Way I See It Now,* have sold fantastically in dozens of countries around the world. I gather it's even been translated into Hebrew!

After the first book was published, a young teacher told me she'd found it really helpful for her remedial class because it was in such plain simple language. I wasn't sure whether to be offended or flattered, but I suppose that's the key to the communication thing. I'm not very academic or intellectual but I do think and reckon I'm reasonably logical. Most people are much the same so I guess it's easier to catch one another's wavelength.

I vividly remember two exceptions, both on Christian platforms and both with student audiences. One was at the Enfield College of Technology and the other at Lancaster University. On both occasions I'd been invited to talk about what I believed and answer questions. On both occasions the students – or rather minority sections of them – had other ideas.

The Enfield meeting was the only time I've ever been really scared on stage and I'm positive it was only the constant prayer SOSs that I sent up which saw me through.

Had the College Christian Union warned us about regular disruption of their meetings by Communists, we may well have had second thoughts about going. But they didn't and, in all innocence, Bill and I powered our way through occasional shouts and barracking, till we arrived at the open question-time. That apparently was what the comrades were waiting for, and suddenly I was on the receiving end of politically-loaded questions which I couldn't understand, let alone answer.

Knowing I was totally out of my depth, all I could do was mentally depend on God to see me through and defend myself against the barrage as best I could. When it was over, the CU Secretary dashed up and, with a great beam, told me it was the first meeting for months that hadn't been physically broken up, and he was thrilled at what I'd said. To this day I don't know what it was, but then I'm pretty sure they weren't my words anyway!

Lancaster University was a different kettle of fish altogether. And that was more frustrating than frightening. Again we were there to talk about Christ and part of the audience were there to cause havoc. This time the Gay Liberation Front were mainly in evidence, infiltrated, I gather, by Rent-a-Mob, made up of various Leftist agitators who did the rounds of public meetings on the university campus.

Nearly 20 years after leaving Cheshunt Secondary School, I went back for an old boys' production of 'Midsummer Night's Dream'. Drama teacher Jay Norris wears the trousers!

I probably learn more from dialogue with students than they learn from me.

Now don't go getting any ideas – it was for a tv sketch!

Little Matilda Mwale from Zambia was brought to
London by Tear Fund for special surgery.

After ten minutes or so, it was obvious that there was little point in carrying on. Short of having the thirty or so chanting shrieking characters physically ejected, which I refused to let happen, it was impossible to make ourselves heard and we called it a day. At least, we did as far as the Gay Lib were concerned.

What we did was to clear the hall and then re-admit the main chunk of the audience, together with a whole crowd outside who hadn't been able to get tickets in the first place. So finally Jesus won the day!

I might add that, when the whole thing was finished, we spoke to one or two of the Gay Lib people who had waited outside and they were really upset at what had happened. Apparently they genuinely wanted to talk about serious things and were prepared to listen, as well as present their case. Regrettably, they admitted, the movement had been infiltrated by a bunch of morons who wanted nothing more than extrovert publicity.

Later I offered to meet a dozen of their representatives, along with five of my friends, on neutral ground in Birmingham. David MacInnes of Birmingham Cathedral agreed to set things up and the only stipulation I made was 'no press'. I never had a reply and I can only assume that their desire to talk was motivated by something other than a sense of need!

My only other encounter with the Gay Lib was during one of the preliminary Festival of Light meetings at Westminster Central Hall in London. I was one of a whole crowd of people, including Malcolm Muggeridge, who were identifying with the Festival, and the Gay Lib and others were there intent on stirring the pot.

It came home to me there more than anywhere else, I think, that there really is a battle being fought and Satan is very much alive and well. And although I had initial reservations about the Festival of Light, that meeting dispelled any doubts about whose side I was on. Despite the opposition, the rally never got out of control and the sense of prayer was fantastic.

Out of the corner of my eye, I remember seeing a little old lady sitting in the audience. Next to her was a burly bloke who every few minutes kept jumping up, yelling and cursing, and shaking his fist. She took it patiently for about twenty minutes, then suddenly got hold of her handbag and gave him such a wallop round the head with it that we never heard another word from him. Prayer evidently wasn't her only weapon!

That rally and the massive turn-out by Christians in Trafalgar Square and Hyde Park a few weeks later were incredible experiences. As far as I'm concerned, what I saw there was proof that love can and does triumph hands-down over evil. The power that radiated from that Jesus crowd was almost a tangible thing and the opposition which had come determined to break everything apart was flummoxed, not by haughty religious condemnation but by outgoing happiness and concern.

'Jesus loves you' was the day's message and was the theme I took up for a song I wrote afterwards about the Festival, and which I've sung a few hundred times since.

My association with the Festival of Light was fairly short-lived really. As I say, I was a hundred per cent part of it at the beginning and its impact, under God, was colossal. But somehow I feel it lost its direction after a couple of years and, although technically I remain on the Council of Reference, nowadays I can hardly call myself an active supporter. Maybe it would have been better to let the original Festival of Light concept, together with its title, phase out naturally once the stand had been made. Any legacy in terms of new project or long-term challenge possibly warranted a new structure and a more apt name.

I'm afraid I was something of a lame duck too on Lord Longford's pornography commission. I had a shrewd idea when I accepted the invitation that I wouldn't be much use but the Festival of Light climate was blowing strong at the time and I genuinely wanted to make the most of every opportunity to put across a balanced Christian viewpoint.

The main problem was that committees turn me into a kind of mute cabbage. I never seem to have anything to contribute that isn't being said already. And if I do come up with an original thought, someone's sure to beat me to it and say it much better! It's not that I'm short of opinions – interviewers know that to their cost – but I find committees stifling and frustrating. The first of the Longford meetings confirmed my misgivings.

A lot of very able people, specialists in this, that and the other, made me feel pretty redundant, although it bothered me that some of them tended to make authoritative statements on morality which bore no relation at all to God's absolutes. To my mind, it's a waste of time theorising about codes of behaviour unless somewhere there's an ultimate right and wrong.

However, many of the members' papers made enlightening reading and there's bound to be some long-term value from the hundreds of hours of research, discussion and writing that busy people volunteered. Certainly if the Commission's work pioneers any legislation which reduces the availability and influence of pornography on society, then I'm glad to at least have given my name to it. Dare I say, though, that I doubt whether it will! As long as the demand exists, so will the supply. Consequently, if we really want to lessen demand, we've got to look beyond laws and penalties to people's natures and, to my knowledge, only Christ can make changes at that level.

At least with the Commission I put in a token attendance. Sadly there must be scores of clubs and organisations which have my name on their letter-heading but which have never seen hide or hair of me. Maybe it helps the work in some way to have a familiar name as patron or vice-president, and, if so, fine. For my part, it's all too easy to dispense my name left, right and centre, and agree to all the requests from well-meaning organisers who believe that a batch of famous evangelical names behind their work will give it an extra status. The danger is that the same names crop up so often that identification becomes not only meaningless but just a wee bit dishonest.

As a rule, unless there is some genuine prospect of my being practically involved every now and again, I tend to turn down invitations like these and, I tell you, the hardest thing is to say 'No'. That's why it's so unfair of people to collar me in the street or at a meeting and ask whether I will attend such-and-such a service or rally on a date yet to be arranged! Usually I don't know what I'm doing next week, let alone in six months' time, so I generally make polite encouraging noises and leave it to Bill to sort out in correspondence. Actually I've landed him in the soup more than once with people who maintain that 'Cliff definitely promised to come' and who are convinced for ever after that I'm surrounded by a group of 'heavies' who really make the decisions. In fact, Bill's a born diplomat and we haven't made that many enemies – at least, if we have he doesn't tell me!

The ever-increasing invitations are an extraordinary assortment. Sunday School anniversaries, university seminars, lunch-time lectures, appeals for the new church roof, and dozens and dozens of inevitable fête and bazaar openings. If I had no career and if there were ten days in a week, I couldn't cope with a quarter of them. Yet virtually every one has its own value or unique opportunity, and discerning priorities is quite a task. Obviously the time factor is a major criterion.

Huge chunks of the year don't allow any extras in the diary. A concert tour, for instance, or a TV series leave few spare hours, and sometimes rehearsal or recording schedules are arranged at such short notice that long-term arrangements are impossible to fix with any degree of certainty.

Yet, despite the schedule hazards, time there certainly is and has to be for at least some of the doors that are open for me, and the most appealing of those doors are churches or fellowships who want me, not as a pew-filler for some one-off morale-boosting spectacular, but as someone who slots into an ongoing, balanced, effective programme of evangelism and teaching.

I know the Spirit of God is able to work anywhere in any situation but, in human terms, I doubt the value of my spending a couple of hours speaking and singing in a kind of spiritual vacuum. All that results from that is a lot of people with a lot of questions, frustrated because local Christians are neither geared, nor able, nor sufficiently committed, to channel them into a Christ-centred, caring, outgoing church.

Most of the meetings we take part in these days present fabulous opportunities. The organisation has been wise and meticulous, and the whole thing has been drenched in prayer for weeks beforehand. Occasionally we meet a minister whose chief concern is to get my autograph in his visitors' book and that's disappointing.

Downright shattering, though, was to find early on that, even within the Christian community, there are the 'con-men' who presumably believe that in evangelism any means justify the end. Don't get me wrong – there aren't many of them and it's inevitable, I suppose, that in every aspect of society there are the fakes and the mentally sick, but the damage that's done can be disastrous.

In the Midlands, for example, a Christian rally was advertised at which I was supposed to sing and speak. Neither I nor Bill knew anything about it; there had been no invitation, no correspondence. The hall was packed and at starting-time there was no Cliff. The chap invented some apology which was bad enough, but incredibly went on to announce that my car had broken down on the motorway and that if people waited I should make it before the close! The whole thing was a huge embarrassment and what it did to the cause of Christ in the area I shudder to think.

Then there was the organiser of Christian concerts who, after inviting me to take part and receiving a 'regret not possible' reply, embarked on a promotion gimmick that would have sent the adrenalin belting through the Trades Description men. It was around the time when 'Congratulations' was being whistled by just about every errand-boy in the country, so our not-so-subtle friend scrambled the letters, concocted a word like 'Tnsgrocualtaion' and asked his readers in the ad to 'guess who's appearing at our next concert'.

Some would say I'm naïve when it comes to sizing up people and their motives – or maybe just plain gullible. Personally that doesn't bother me and I much prefer taking people at their face value. Again, though, I'm in the fortunate position of not having to worry. Friends and colleagues are much better at discerning the fakes and the would-be exploiters.

Other people, I find, are much more aware of this odd celebrity status thing than I am, and it's they who are determined to slot me into some different category to other mortals. It amuses me, for instance, when churches write to invite me to participate in a service and ask what my fee is! It's a question they'd never dream of putting to a Christian speaker who might be a teacher or a missionary or a builder – so why put it to me?

Now, I'm not complaining – the question is right and proper – for the labourer, we're told, is worthy of his hire. The point is that we're not consistent and, because I am well-known, I'm given a consideration over and above Joe Bloggs and, Christian brethren, that ain't right! Incidentally, I wonder what reaction I'd get if I wrote back to the church and said there was my usual professional fee!

I've always had a romantic hankering after a student kind of existence – not the academic side, you understand, more the cloisters, the common-room, and the gown and mortar-board!

Maybe there was a bit of that behind the anticipation of two months' study at Oak Hill Theological College near Barnet.

The year before, I asked Peter Gormley, my manager, to clear the diary and, as always, that was no sooner said than done. More seriously, I felt the need for some kind of formal Bible study, in view of all the pummelling I was getting from people around the country who wanted my advice on everything from Christian philosophy through to their personal and domestic problems.

Whether I liked it or not, I had to face the extraordinary fact that there were people who viewed me as some sort of authority on God and who were more ready to listen to me than the church establishment. Now I know the only authority I have is based on God's word and my experience, and I'm the last to be deluded into thinking that I've got any more right than the next man to stand up in public and spout my opinions. But the difference was that people were asking me and not the next man, and so I reckoned I had a responsibility to give them the best I was capable of.

Besides that, I felt a very personal need for more Bible intake. Most Sundays I was out and about, taking part in services in Anglican churches, Brethren halls and Baptist chapels, and was conscious of being on a starvation diet myself.

The staff at Oak Hill were fabulous and, instead of sitting in on mid-course lectures with all the budding clergy, I was treated to private tutorials by a team of top scholars who were willing to stoop uncommonly low to communicate on my level!

It's difficult to assess the outcome of that course or to put my finger on any one specific result. I know I valued it enormously and that, after an interview I did for the BBC, David Winter mentioned that my answers had become noticeably more succinct. For my own good, it's crucial that I venture into the student world again – and soon!

9 Maintaining a Career

IF YOU'VE GOT the idea that divine guidance is some tidy packaged formula which, once discovered, steers the Christian effortlessly through life's complexities, then forget it! In my experience, the direction we're given is usually to a very small scale. The essentials are there but the details, the every-day decisions and judgments, are left for us to work at and to fathom out.

So while, on the one hand, I can refer confidently to God guiding my career, I'm equally aware, on the other, of my responsibility to maintain it, and that involves hard work and painful mistakes. Recording 'Honky Tonk Angel' was one of them – but I'll save that till later!

As soon as I aligned myself with evangelical Christianity, there were two interesting interpretations. Some saw it as a gimmick, a clever piece of image-building concocted by the PR men to broaden my appeal. And there were those who viewed it as professional suicide – the same ones who predicted the flight of fans after the Billy Graham stand. I suppose both reactions are understandable, though I guess those who still believe that it's all a gimmick, even after eleven years, must be marginally prejudiced!

Maybe the predictions of professional disaster acted as a kind of challenge. Maybe they underestimated the intelligence and integrity of the public. Whatever the reason, I'm relieved they proved false and that, in concerts at home and overseas, we went on playing to packed audiences. Records continued to sell well around the world; TV series achieved high viewing ratings; and, most gratifying of all, my audience seemed to span an incredible age range, from kids in junior school through to one old lady who, at ninety-eight, must be 'queen of the ravers'.

One of the trophies I'm proud of most, and which hangs in my music room at home, is a framed copy of an advertisement which impresario Leslie Grade published in the showbiz press a few years ago, congratulating the cast of the Cliff Richard Show on breaking all box-office records at the London Palladium. The fact that that happened to me as a Christian was a tremendous encouragement and put the prophets of doom into some perspective. The point was that, as a Christian entertainer, I had to be better than I was before. Standards had to be that much higher, preparation and rehearsal that much more conscientious. 'Whatever you do,' says one of those main-route Bible directives, 'do it to the glory of Christ.' And that applies to an artist in show-business as much as to a secretary in commerce, a student in college, or a vicar in church.

One of the objections I still meet quite often is from the Christian who, in all sincerity, feels compelled to write me off as a Christian brother because of my involvement in show-business. Except for the sad few who condemn themselves far more than me by their bitterness, most seem genuinely at a loss to understand how I can identify with a profession which in itself, they presumably believe, contradicts Christian ethics.

Like so many areas of tension, the problem is one of misunderstanding more than fundamental conflict. And when, all too rarely, I get the opportunity to talk the thing through with someone on a personal level, the problem seems to melt away. The basic answer of course is that show-business is neutral. Music, laughter and entertainment are valid ingredients of God's creation, and therefore the theatre is no more sinful than the people who comprise it. Put another way, it's no more and no less sinful than any other business or any other profession, and I've yet to hear anyone query whether it's permissible for a Christian to direct a company or work in a bank! Besides, if there were such a thing as a 'holy' job which grabbed all the Christians, who's going to act as salt in all the 'unholy' ones?

But maybe that's another subject. One of the complaints I share with a lot of showbiz people is that I talk a great deal and, whilst that's an asset for chat shows and interviews, it usually makes for a bad listener. I know I'd be lousy at any kind of personal counselling and would be butting in with answers before I'd heard the questions. But everyone to his own thing, and frequent invitations to take part in dialogue or discussion shows of one kind or another have provided fabulous platforms. Personally I don't think it's the Christian commitment itself which interests producers but evidence of the growing-up which it sparked off. Instead of narrowing my vision, my conversion broadened it vastly, and a lot of the blinkers I used to wear dropped away as I got progressively more involved in various Christian activities. I found myself, for the first time, thinking seriously about some of the newsy issues of the day, and the whole business of my responsibilities as an entertainer took on new significance.

Maybe it's staid old age creeping on – I don't know – but it honestly beats me when some of our current teenybopper favourites maintain that their stage act has no real effect on anyone. To my mind, everything we do on stage as artists is done to achieve some kind of effect. If I'm singing a love song, I want to affect people emotionally; if it's a song about pollution, I want them to think, 'Ugh, he's right'; if they are Jesus lyrics, then I'd like people to know that I believe them. Each song communicates in its own way and, if there were no effect, I wouldn't waste time singing it.

Similarly, I don't see how a twelve- or fourteen-year-old youngster can watch an act of simulated violence, even in the context of pop, and not be affected in some way by it. We may think we've shoved this or that experience aside but it's there in our subconscious, part and parcel of the people we are.

In a way, I'm in a fortunate position, I suppose, for no one is likely to let me forget that I've a standard to maintain. One slightly doubtful joke or lyric and the next week's mail would be full of letters from triumphant critics: '. . . and you call yourself a Christian!' In actual fact, I don't have to do much vetting of scripts or lyrics these days. Other people do it on my behalf!

One TV producer was so protective that he thought I shouldn't say, 'Oh blimey' in one particular sketch. Before I saw it, he blue-pencilled the 'Oh blimey', and there was the substitute – 'Oh dear'.

The only time I've had any serious confrontation regarding the content of a show was at the beginning of one concert tour. After the first house, one of my musicians warned me that I'd better listen to the warm-up comedian. During the next house I stood in the wings and heard the bluest and sickest material I think I have ever heard, either on stage or off it. I visualised all the parents out front who had brought their kids to watch what they trusted would be decent entertainment. It was my show and they were my responsibility. What I did was professionally distasteful and maybe unethical, but I still feel there was no option but to 'phone my agent and say that either the comedian left or I did. There was no way that we could share the same bill. The next day he was replaced. Ironically, since then, that same comedian has gone on to achieve star status.

But let's get the balance right. Protest has its place but too much time and energy is easily spent complaining about what's wrong rather than doing what's right. The negative caricature of Christianity which the media love to highlight is a travesty of what it's actually about. The problem nowadays is that we seem to have got so accustomed to built-in innuendo in entertainment that our judgment has gone up the spout.

I remember one national newspaper critic writing of one of my TV shows that it was so wholesome, it made him sick! Fair enough, he didn't enjoy it – that's his freedom, but it seems a sinister indication of our age when good and bad swop places.

I'm very conscious that my TV shows go into millions of homes and that

The glamour of show-biz! Overnight travel on a
Japanese 'sleeper' is an experience I don't recommend.
Peering out of their respective shelves are Bruce
Welch and guitarist Terry Britten. Pianist and clown,
Cliff Hall, is still on his feet.

there are thousands of young kids watching. I want to show them that it's possible to entertain, be with it, sing hip songs, and maintain Christian values at the same time. If that makes some folk sick, well, I guess they deserve to be. Happily, a good many viewers have told the BBC that they welcome a show which they can watch as a family, knowing beforehand that they won't be embarrassed.

The gospel numbers that I inject into my stage concerts also upset some of the critics. 'The inevitable gospel slot' was how one writer cynically demolished it. But again, to my mind, it would be dishonest not to include some gospel material in my act because on stage I'm me! I can't stop being a Christian the minute I walk into the 'Talk of the Town'. The audience come to see my performance and there's no way I can sever my Christian beliefs from it.

The main criterion I apply in selecting that gospel section is its ability to stand up musically. There's no question of including it merely for the sake of 'having something religious'! The material must be professionally acceptable and, whereas a few years back that would have excluded just about everything on the Christian music scene, today some really brilliant Christian musicians and songwriters have emerged. If you doubt it, grab a Larry Norman or a Randy Stonehill album and hear what I mean!

And again, as a performer, I want to affect my audience on as many levels as possible, so why ignore the spiritual? It's as much part of our make-up as anything else although, admittedly, generally a bit more dormant. A moment or two of spiritual awareness is a valid audience experience.

Some, of course, claim that that's indoctrination; usually they're the people who've never seen me in concert and presume I do nothing but push religion. I've already told you what I think of Christian 'indoctrination'; it's a contradiction in terms. Christianity starts with an individual encountering Jesus and that can never be humanly engineered. But naturally, like everyone else, I must use my platform fairly and we take great pains in our advertising to distinguish between what are specifically gospel concerts and what is predominantly pop. The important factor is that people should know what they're paying for. If we mislead or take advantage of an audience, then we deserve all we get.

What did surprise me was that when we performed in Moscow and Leningrad for three weeks in 1976 the Russians raised no objections to the gospel numbers. After all I'd heard about censorship and the authorities' religious sensitivity, I was sure we would run into deep water. I couldn't have been more wrong. We even included 'When I survey the wondrous cross' and no one so much as turned a hair! Mind you, if they had demanded any kind of cut, I'd have backed out of the whole project. As it happened, the only lyric they took exception to in the whole act was a line from 'Love Train', one of the 'Philly sound' numbers. One verse refers to people in Russia, China and Israel joining hands and that, I think, may have been misinterpreted as politically loaded!

Before we took off for Russia, we really hadn't a clue what we were in for. The invitation to perform had come from the official State Entertainments Department – Gosconcerts – who had obviously decided that our music was 'culturally acceptable' for Russian youth. Apparently I was the first western 'pop-rock' artist to be declared blemish-free, but I looked upon the prospect with a jaundiced eye and wouldn't have cared in the least if plans had collapsed at the last minute.

In the end, I was so glad they didn't. The people who warned us about the reserve of the Moscow audience, the likelihood of elderly officials outnumbering the youngsters, were way off beam. Every one of the twenty concerts, in fact, was sold out weeks before we arrived, and rumour had it that touts were making a fortune selling tickets on the sly at forty or fifty pounds apiece.

The audiences were fantastic – warm, friendly and so appreciative that after the first night in Leningrad we had to open up the orchestra pit to deter enormous bearded Russians from leaping on stage to give us bear-hugs! It was the same in Moscow. Again, no question of polite genteel applause but excitement and wild appreciation reminiscent of the Glasgow dates in the early 'sixties – well, almost! Scores of people were out of their seats, clamouring down the aisles in a mood of sheer honest enjoyment. There were no rowdies, no violence, just people letting their hair down together in what was obviously a new musical experience.

Some days later newsmen from the Russian agency, Tass, reported the country's 'first real taste of Western rock 'n roll' and they were as flattering with their praise and acclamation as any press I have had the world over.

There is no way I can knock Russia on the basis of that tour. I'm all for taking people as you find them and I found them cooperative, friendly and anxious to please. Of course there may have been ulterior motives and the whole exercise could have been ingenious window-dressing. But, rightly or wrongly, I take things as I find them and all I know is that for three weeks I was allowed a free hand to communicate my music, to speak about Jesus, and even to worship with fellow-believers in the Moscow Baptist Church. In each respect language was a difficulty but not once was it a barrier. In the theatres we were at one musically; in Christ I sensed with believers a much deeper unity spiritually.

It surprised me to find that Moscow Baptist Church packed in not just one Sunday congregation but three – one in the morning, one in the

The Easter Broads cruise is a highlight for Finchley Crusaders.

After 20 minutes playing in a charity football match at
Southall, I needed a breather, so the ref was primed
to show me to the dressing-room.

OPPOSITE Two of the most talented guitarists around –
Bryn Haworth and Terry Britten.

afternoon, and yet another in the evening. Despite two shows on the Saturday and a ridiculously late night, I struggled out to the ten o'clock service, feeling immensely sacrificial, and found the place jammed. Fortunately a special pew was kept for visitors and I was ushered in. It wasn't until we stood for the first hymn that I noticed there were no hymn-books – well, there were some – as far as I could see, about one between twenty. I gathered later that there were strict laws regulating all printed material. As hymnbooks and Bibles fell apart with use and age, they were well-nigh impossible to replace. A couple of evenings earlier a Russian poet told me at an Embassy reception that he had only been permitted a very limited edition of his own writings, and literature of all kinds was carefully monitored and controlled.

But it would have taken more than a ban on hymn-books to dampen the worship and enthusiasm of those believers. After each verse the minister halted the singing and read out aloud the following verse. I couldn't understand a word but, with memories refreshed, everyone launched forth again with a vigour and a joy that I couldn't help comparing to the feeble efforts of so many of our own church congregations. I wondered who were the more free!

Then they came to 'What a Friend we have in Jesus' – at least, I presume it was. The tune was the same so I croaked happily away in English, for the first time feeling more than just a spectator. After a fabulous choir had sung the anthem, my heart sank when I saw the choir-master making a beeline straight for me. Before the service he'd asked if I'd sing something but I'd explained how nothing melodious seemed to come out of my throat early in the morning and that I'd rather not. Maybe he was a good psychologist, I don't know, but I think he knew I couldn't refuse again. I really wanted to be part of that service and he sensed that I did. Sure enough: 'I just wondered if you'd changed your mind about singing,' he whispered loudly in English. I had, and from the packed balcony of Moscow Baptist Church I sang a very husky, but for me never more emotional

> 'When I survey the wondrous cross
> on which the Prince of Glory died,
> my richest gain I count but loss,
> and pour contempt on all my pride.'

As I breathed virtually the first note into the microphone, everyone stood up – old men and women, younger people, a handful of soldiers – all of them stood silent and still, and in those three short minutes our understanding of one another was perfect. Language didn't matter.

Cultural differences and lifestyles were irrelevant. In Jesus we were one family. And if that puzzles you, then I can't begin to find adequate words to convey the reality and the depth of that experience. The best I can do is urge that you discover for yourself.

Add to that the fact that Soviet Christians were glad and encouraged simply that I went, that one public figure had made a public stand in their own country, *on their side* – then there is no question. If the invitation's renewed, I'll be back, bugs or no bugs!

There were those at home who said I should never have gone to Russia, that by working there I was condoning official policies, even supporting censorship and persecution. It's an opinion I don't share. No problem is solved by isolating oneself from it and, although I don't pretend that those three weeks contributed anything very significant to international relations, I'm idealist enough to hope that a bridge may have been set up here and there which couldn't have happened if I'd stayed at home.

Anyway, back to the plot and to that all-important business of keeping musically 'fresh'.

One of the factors which I'm sure has helped to keep my career on the boil has been my reluctance to be trapped into one kind of musical 'bag'. Whereas some artists have made their mark only with protest songs, folk songs, rock'n roll, or reggae, my career has been littered with all manner of material. In the same way, although I know my main appeal is to a family audience, I don't really want to limit my audience to any one label or grouping.

That's why, for me, one of the most satisfying TV programmes I've done recently was one of the 'In concert' shows. That's a series which features artists singing material which they themselves have written or which has made them famous over the years. Usually they're fairly in-crowd people such as David Gates, or Crosby, Stills, Nash & Young. For ages I wanted to do that show, if only to sing stuff that I liked and to show that my own taste was broader than 'Living Doll' and 'Congratulations'.

By musical standards I'm no great guitarist but it was a rare opportunity to show off the limited ability I do have. Oddly enough, it was my conversion that caused me to take the guitar seriously again. I'd been pretty inept in the early days and the expensive Jumbo Gibson I owned had been collecting moths at the bottom of a cupboard. What point was there in bothering with a guitar when Hank Marvin was around? But at Christian meetings Hank wasn't around and it was taken for granted that I'd sing. There was no option. The Jumbo came out of the cupboard and I had to fumble my own accompaniment.

Happily I've improved a hundred per cent since then and can bluff most people into thinking I can play. Most people, that is, except Hank and good guitarists! Maybe that 'In concert' programme was a big ego trip for me but I loved it none the less!

In the old days I detested television work. What threw me most was having to cope with a studio audience and simultaneously perform to a camera. Shows that went out live were murderous and for a while I threw a moody and insisted on no studio audiences. Today we've struck a happy medium – recorded, rather than live, shows and as big a studio audience as the producer wants! In that way there's no tension, no ghastly finality about a fluffed line or a faulty note.

In our programme I tried the Cat Stevens hit 'Morning has broken' and I just couldn't get the lyrics right. The first fluff embarrassed me, the second embarrassed the audience, at the third effort we started to laugh, and by the fifth time round the whole studio was in hysterics. Eventually we made it, but that freedom, almost like a film set, is my kind of atmosphere.

I realise I'm fortunate in having got to a position where I can expect the facility to do something again and again till it's right. I know too well that I'm not always capable of being spot on in my singing, but I do like things to be as right as we can possibly make them. And, to my mind, whether you're playing to millions through television or to a thousand in a concert hall, you have a responsibility to make the performance one hundred per cent professional. And that goes for musicians and technicians as well as for me.

I'm particularly fussy about sound and assume that when people pay to see me on stage they want me to sound like my records. In the past that was virtually impossible but nowadays, with all the technological advances in sound systems, it's possible to put a microphone on every instrument, just as you would in a recording studio. Of course acoustics are never as good but, even so, the result is a fair copy of what's achieved on record.

A few times, after a stage show, people have asked me if I was miming and, in a way, that's a backhanded compliment. In fact, we spend hours every day of a concert tour checking sound balances. Every hall has its own sound idiosyncrasies and the sound setting for one hall doesn't mean it's right for the next. Some theatres are diabolical for sound, and the fact that we achieve a reasonable standard at all is due in large measure to the experience and patience of David Bryce, who for years now has been my touring manager.

David must be known and respected by the technical staff of just about every concert hall in the country. He's one of those characters who inspire an uncanny sort of confidence. If he's around then somehow, even amidst the most awful muddle, you know everything will be fine by curtain call. I can't conceive now of going on tour without him, and his bald head and stocky figure have become a sort of professional attachment. I often refer on stage to the two old ladies who saw David and me out together in some northern town. (You must remember that David, with the original Kojak hairstyle, doesn't look like me one bit.) One lady spotted us, nudged the other and whispered, 'Look, dear, there's that Cliff Richard.' 'Oh,' said the other, screwing her eyes up, 'which one?'

David's all-round talents, involving handling press, stage management, directing sound and lighting, getting me in and out of theatres, and a hundred and one other things I usually take for granted, have been acquired over years in the business. From the time he and his brother, Dickie Valentine, were call-boys at the Prince of Wales Theatre, David has managed to absorb the skills of the job and steer clear of the fake and the froth. There aren't too many characters around who have his kind of integrity.

Just as we pay more attention to our sound systems, I'm increasingly critical of my own singing technique. Maybe it's the age thing again but I've discovered, since doing a two-hour stage act, that there's no need to rush out on stage, grab the audience in the first two songs, prance around like an idiot, and be totally out of breath by the third song and sing it badly. Far better to take your time and build up to the gymnastics later.

I've always regarded my singing voice as little more than a natural extension of speaking and I've never gone in for any formal voice training or singing practice. Rightly or wrongly, I feel freer, more at ease, just singing the way it comes. For a few minutes I can manage a passable impersonation of Harry Secombe but I could never sustain it, and that kind of contrived operatic style involves a completely different technique and approach.

I have a very small voice in fact, and without a microphone people would barely hear me in the front row. That'll make a few purists look down their noses but a microphone style involves a skill of its own and, for my money, gives a much greater sensitivity in vocal sound.

What I do recognise as a weakness is my inability to read a note of music, although in defence I argue again that my singing comes totally naturally and even learning a tune from a set of dots has a contrived ring about it. The problem, if that's the right word, is that if I hear a song and like it, I can learn it very easily. They call it a natural ear and, given that, the pop world serves the rest up on a plate.

In the old days, it was in the form of a hack pianist who would thump out the tune that had to be learned, as many times as necessary. Recently it's by way of a demo tape which is often better than the record which follows!

It goes back, I suppose, to my childhood hang-up of not bothering with things that didn't interest me. Basically I'm not much interested in learning music; I don't feel the need for it and there's no incentive.

But acting – that's something else. Way before 'Two a Penny' I had an ambition to act – seriously, I mean, not the knockabout extension of Cliff Richard in 'Summer Holiday' and 'The Young Ones' but serious legit acting. I know, by the limited experience I've had already on stage and by 'Two a Penny', that I can do it. The problem is to convince others that I can!

My two professional excursions so far into straight stage acting were both with the Bromley Repertory Company, and maybe the most historical event of that chapter was that we closed the Bromley New Theatre! It burnt down four days before we were due to open in *The Potting Shed*. I remember waking one morning during the last week of rehearsals, turning on the radio, and hearing a traffic report warning motorists to avoid Bromley High Street because of fire. 'Funny if it was the theatre,' I thought. It was. Ten minutes later there was a 'phone call – no rehearsal, no play, no theatre.

Just as I started forgetting lines, the 'phone rang again. An Indian dancing troupe had cancelled a week's booking at Sadler's Wells; if we chopped back the scenery and breathed in, we could just about wedge ourselves in. What did I think? There was no question. It might be the one and only chance of a West End acting debut.

To our relief and delight, we got reasonable reviews, did excellent business, but by the time we'd got ourselves organised as a cast, the whole project was over. Four weeks' rehearsal for one week's season. Despite the chaos, it was a great experience. There was a strange sense of achievement in being able to communicate powerfully on a level so different from the one I was used to. Undoubtedly it did me good to be stretched for once and to accept the discipline of being one of a team. If I hadn't got the acting bug good and proper before *The Potting Shed*, I suffered it afterwards. It remains to be seen whether there'll be future symptoms. I have a shrewd feeling there might be.

TOP LEFT 'Got a good opening line?' Hurried preparation before Bill Latham and I launch into after-dinner dialogue.

TOP RIGHT Sight-seeing in Russia with our interpreter, Genrietta, and my travelling manager, David Bryce.

CENTRE LEFT Tear Fund has supported hundreds of folk on short-term assignments around the world. With George Hoffman is physiotherapist, Jennie Collins.

CENTRE RIGHT Opportunities crop up all over the world to sing and speak about Jesus. This was in Katmandu, Nepal.

BOTTOM My respect for Dr. Billy Graham grows with every meeting. This was in Brussels.

10 Perks of Pop

I FEEL REALLY SORRY for people who dread Mondays. The thought of having to cope with a tedious irritating job day after day is horrific, and I often wonder what would have happened to me as a person if I'd been forced to spend twenty years as a clerk in Atlas Lamps on the Great Cambridge Road. It's daft, but there are times when I feel almost guilty for enjoying my job so much and getting paid for it into the bargain! Mondays are a kind of extension to the weekend and if there's a week of exhausting rehearsal ahead I'm able to relish even that.

It's because of my own enjoyment that I tend to be a bit cynical about those usually jaded artists who do their best to convince the public that it's 'tough at the top'. You know the kind of thing you read in the press – that the pressures and demands are so great that alcohol, drugs, break-up of relationships and breakdown of health are inevitable, and that stars are actually victims to be pitied. Frankly, I don't believe it. Of course, some have cracked and warrant our sympathy and, fair enough, it's true in any profession that the higher up the ladder you climb the more demanding are the responsibilities. But let's be honest – it's a good deal tougher at the bottom!

I have even less time for the other old chestnut – the 'fame hasn't changed me' line. Take that again with a generous pinch of salt. Personally I'm miles off being convinced that a high income and a position in the public eye don't have an automatic effect on attitudes and life-style. I can only use my experience. While in one sense I don't regard myself as a big spender and want to use the money I have as responsibly as I can, it's true also that I do eat out quite frequently in pricey restaurants. I appreciate good food, well-prepared, in pleasant surroundings. It's a fact that I run a comfortable car which enables me to do a five-hour haul up the motorway for a concert without feeling whacked at the end.

And it's a fact that the house I live in, with its music-room extension, acre of garden – nearly all rhododendrons and azaleas – and swimming-pool, is, to my mind, perfection. At home I can get away from the cranks, the autograph-hunters and the merely curious. Outside, among the trees, I can look up at nothing but sky, walk my dog safely round the golf-course, and there's no one to invade the privacy which I value so highly. For me that's real therapy.

But if all that's not a change from cycling to work from a council-house in Cheshunt, I don't know what is. Of course things are different, profoundly different, and that's proved a trouble some irritant for a number of people. Success in one's career and a Christian commitment are somehow mutually exclusive, or at least that's what some would have me believe. The part of the Bible that I'm confronted with more than any other, I think, is Jesus' teaching about the rich man, the camel, and the eye of the needle.

'How do you reconcile that?' people ask, often, regrettably, with a hint of hostility, and assuming I've never thought about it before. If they mean 'how do I get round it?' the short answer is that I don't. One of the most futile exercises is to try to force God's teaching to fit our circumstances instead of vice versa – allowing our circumstances to be shaped by God's teaching.

That doesn't mean, though, that we duck out of reality. We do live in a material world with our possessions, and what I have tried to do is to see wealth the way God sees it. I know that's a highminded thing to say but it's what I mean. When I first became a Christian, it upset me that I was famous and wealthy because I couldn't see how I could live life as a Christian and be this fortunate. This is one of the reasons I wanted to get out and be 'ordinary'.

But the accounts of Solomon and David in the Old Testament helped me understand another perspective. You see, although they were wealthy, they both at some stages of their lives pleased God. The fact that they had possessions enough to make Paul Getty seem a pauper didn't disqualify them from a relationship with God. It was when Solomon got his priorities mixed and his earthly treasures became more important to him than obedience to God that things turned sour. That's the danger of course and, believe me, I'm well aware of it.

My responsibility – and everyone has a similar responsibility on this score – is to discover how God wants me to use my time and my finance, and to do that I must rely on the fact that God does give clear direction. If God were to make it clear to me that I should relinquish my career and my finance, then I would be prepared to do it – or, rather, I think I would. There's a world of difference, I know, between talking and doing.

What bothers me – admittedly not so much now as it used to – is that other people, Christians or not, try to rush me into situations at the speed they want me to go. From the moment I was converted, some wanted a kind of spectacular martyrdom, maybe subconsciously to bolster their own faith. I was expected to give up my career, give up my money, give up my fame, all in one go. Well, all right, maybe after I've been a Christian a few more years, I'll reach a point where I feel it's right to do all that. At the moment I don't believe it is.

My reading of Scripture is that God doesn't intend us to adopt a kind of refugee-camp existence. If we say that Christians shouldn't be wealthy, then where do we draw the line? What is wealthy? What's poor? And what's normal? Compared to the average Bengali in Bangladesh, there's barely a single person in Britain, including those on the dole, who isn't a millionaire hundreds of times over. Fifty per cent or more unemployed, men working for the equivalent of tenpence a day (if they're lucky) – how do you begin to compare that with any situation at home? We make the mistake of saying that so-and-so earns forty pounds a week so he is forty pounds guilty of being rich; she earns sixty pounds so she's sixty pounds guilty. It's an argument that gets us nowhere fast.

Personally my current concern is to be rid of some of the complexities which gum up my finances and which prevent the kind of flexibility I'd like to have with my money. You'd never believe, for instance, what a problem it's been to tithe my income. I still don't fully understand why but it's something to do with the erratic unpredictable way it comes in. I couldn't force the experts to do what they told me was impractical so I now work on the principle of setting a chunk of my earning time aside so that cash can flow in other directions.

You'll have gathered I'm pretty clueless when it comes to business affairs, and in general I leave that whole area to a very efficient accountant crew. Every so often I get a message to 'tighten the belt' or the more subtle approach, 'You'll notice, Cliff, that outgoings are a little up on last year . . .'

Actually I was reading a press article the other day about how the stars are supposed to live. Gold taps in the bathroom, Greek sculpture in the gym, and priceless art treasures in the loo are the norm apparently, and if you can boast an indoor aviary of exotic birds and drink champagne and orange juice for breakfast, you qualify for superstar status. In nine cases out of ten of course, it's all rubbish, part of the myth which has grown up around a showbiz élite and which some of the public are gullible enough to believe.

The nearest I've come to it is the couple of years I spent at Rookswood, a huge house set in eleven acres in Nazeing. With its panelling from Hampton Court, tasteful Louis XIV lounge, and sweeping lawns, it was well on the way to matching the image. I remember one family we discovered picnicking in the rose-garden indignantly maintaining that it was a public park and they had every right to be there!

But, for all its magnificence, it was never home. Several of the rooms were hardly used and the whole place was a security nightmare. I don't think either my sisters or mother were sorry when we went our separate ways and settled down in proper 'home-size' houses.

The house I had in Portugal was a similar story. Not that this one was outrageously big – the problem here was that it was ludicrously under-used. I think I must have spent only about fifteen or sixteen weeks there in all during the eight years I owned it and, although friends and relatives went there for the occasional fortnight's holiday, it was certainly empty for most of the year. Mind you, every holiday I spent there was fabulous.

The house really wasn't much to shout about but the setting was perfect, if you didn't mind overlooking a cemetery! Actually I think my management were among the first showbiz lot to discover Albufeira and several of us invested money in property at what even at that time were incredibly low prices. Since then, the whole Algarve coast has woken up to its tourist potential and dozens of stage artists from Britain have become Algarve addicts.

Even though I sold the house, I value many friends in and around Albufeira and, despite its inevitable change and development, I still rate it as one of my favourite holiday spots. The sun is guaranteed, there are virtually empty beaches if you take the trouble to drive for five minutes away from town, and there's a hard-to-describe glow about the atmosphere that makes you feel good.

Some of my most glorious relaxed moments have been sitting on the balcony of the villa at about seven in the evening, watching the rocks of the coastline turning a warm golden colour as the sun goes down. The fierce heat of the day is over, the last of the sun-bathers are ambling back for an evening meal and, with a glass of wine and a bowl of peanuts, what more could you want?

For years now a gang of us have teamed up for a summer holiday with grim single-mindedness – to unwind, lie in the sun, and forget 'phones, time schedules and work responsibilities. It's like opening a valve as far as I'm concerned and watching the gradual decrease of pressure. The problem is that the gang – Christian friends from various walks of life – is getting fewer. One by one they drop out of the running, lured away by newly-discovered fiancées. One can only assume that they've weighed their decisions carefully!

One of the perks of show-business that, to a certain extent, is wasted on me is travel. This year alone my passport has been stamped by officials in America, Japan, Hong Kong, Russia, India, Bangladesh and at least half a dozen European neighbours.

'What marvellous opportunities you get for seeing the world!' they say and I feel positively guilty about not sharing their enthusiasm. The fact is that basically I'm not a sightseer. Except for Israel, I've never been turned on one little bit by old buildings, crumbling churches or ancient monuments. Museums and art galleries I view as places of mild punishment, and I confess with some embarrassment that I gave up a visit to the Grand Canyon in favour of watching a floor show at Las Vegas.

Let me add in defence that it was a decision fully endorsed by 'the gang' – one of whom, the biggest rogue of the lot, sits as a JP on a local bench of magistrates.

There's another convenient excuse that's particularly handy for explaining to outraged lovers of relics and the like, who are ready to write me off as an ignorant Philistine and fool. The fact is that it's much less hassle to stay put in an hotel room than to risk an unknown public outside. Airports, hotels and theatres we can describe in every detail; even the roads in between we could manage blindfold, but that's about the extent of it. On tour there's rarely the time, the opportunity or (ssh!) the inclination to see more.

Actually I mustn't paint too black a picture. I do appreciate beautiful scenery very much indeed, as a thousand or more transparencies which I've taken of trees against skies and close-ups of flowers will prove. If I had a choice between town or country living, there'd be no contest. Rural life wins hands down.

Perhaps I'm just a bit perverse and places which people tell me I ought to see for this or that reason never appeal so much. It's not that I'm even anti old buildings. In Oxford, for instance, I'm always knocked out by some of the fabulous architecture and wonder if the students really appreciate it as much as I do. I love the fact that a building is old and solid and stable and looks beautiful, yet for all that I wouldn't cross the road to see and be told that this is where someone sat or was buried or whatever.

Another possession that was comparatively short-lived was a boat. Nothing sea-going or too 'gin-and-Jaguar', you understand, but a safe and very functional six-berth fibre-glass cabin cruiser. My appetite was whetted by the Easter Norfolk Broads trips and for two or three years the Crusader class was able to hire three boats instead of four, making the cost of the holiday for the boys much lower. But again there was the problem of high maintenance costs and comparatively little use over the season.

Even when I moved near to the Thames and had the boat brought down and moored only ten minutes' drive away, I still didn't get the chance to use it properly. The most beautiful stretches of the Thames, I'm told, are beyond Reading into Cotswold country – well, I never once made it that far. By the time we chugged to Windsor, it was about turn and full throttle back home. Naturally other people used it, but after the engine burnt out, the gear smashed, the electrics failed, and I received a stern warning from the river authorities, threatening a summons if a barbecue was used on deck again, I called it a day and got rid of it.

The best perks of all, of course, are those that aren't for sale, like the gilt-edged invitation I had to lunch with the Royal Family. I could hardly believe it. I'd met members of the Royal Family before, at Command Performances and the like, but a handshake and a greeting is one thing; visiting their home for lunch is another.

I owned a Jensen motor-car at the time and had it spit and polished, with chauffeur to match – at least I'd make a good entrance!

The car stopped at the edge of a red-carpeted staircase and I was wafted up into a fabulous olde-worlde room with massive gilt fireplaces and enormous oak antique furniture. I asked the butler, or whoever he was, if it was very old; I'm glad I asked, if only to catch the best withering look I've ever seen. There was a superbly measured pause before the equally withering reply: 'I should hope so, young man.'

There were nine guests – a mixture of people from all kinds of professions – and over a sherry I was trying to work out what, if anything, we had in common. I never did discover.

What bothered me most was the table plan. According to the sketch, it was a long table with rounded ends and, blow me, if my name wasn't stuck at one of the ends. It had to be a mistake – surely the Queen would sit at one end, opposite the Duke. I kept wandering over to check that I'd read it right. Sure enough, all the other names, with strings of letters after them, were along each side. 'Cliff Richard, Singer' was conspicuous at one end!

While I was wondering if I was about to make another more ghastly gaffe, our sherry-sipping was interrupted by a fanfare – not trumpets or any of that film nonsense, but by the snuffling and scuffling of the haughtiest-looking pack of Corgis you can imagine. Hard on their heels were our hosts. If it was stage-managed, it couldn't have been more effective; as an ice-breaker, it was brilliant.

The formalities were few and, as we kept a Corgi, Shandy, at home at that time – a far more beautiful and friendly animal, I might add – we had common ground from the word go.

The table plan turned out to be right. I remember holding back to see whether anyone else went to my place at the end. No one did. The Queen and Prince Philip sat facing each other in the middle, and Princess Anne was next to me on my right. The whole thing was charming and dignified

and I can't imagine an event like it happening anywhere other than in Britain.

The main course was rib of lamb, with peas, carrots, potatoes and gravy, with brandy snaps to follow. Admittedly, the brandy snaps were a bit hard but I did a double-take at Princess Anne when she started whacking at them with a spoon. Now maybe that's how you deal with brandy snaps in posh places, I don't know.

All the Princess muttered by way of explanation was that it was the best way to get at the cream, which, when you think about it, seems perfectly logical. If she did happen to wallop too hard and the things exploded over the carpet, there were always the Corgis hovering around her ankles to remove the evidence.

I discovered afterwards that the chief pastry-maker at the Palace was a pupil at none other than Cheshunt Secondary Modern just a year ahead of me. Two former students making the Palace can't be bad – Eton watch out!

On the dot of three, the flow of chat ended and our hosts withdrew for another appointment. On the way out through the Palace gates, I practised a Royal wave to a bunch of American tourists – it made their day!

It's funny how you imagine other people's places to look like, isn't it? I had this very grandiose idea about Buckingham Palace and it more than lived up to it. I was introduced to a girl recently who imagined that my house was full of awards – walls of gold and silver discs, and stacks of silver bowls and cups displayed all over the place in specially-built cabinets. She must have been horribly disillusioned to hear that one of the few cups on view was in the downstairs loo and contained the spare toilet rolls!

I've got an odd attitude to awards really. I'm thrilled to get them and over the course of the years I've received something like thirty silver discs, eight gold ones, and literally dozens and dozens of plaques, salvers, trays and goodness knows what else, for winning various pop polls. One year – 1966, I think it was – I even got a fabulous gold cup for the ludicrous title of 'World's No 1 Male Singer'. It was an award that Elvis had consistently won and the only reason I took it was that everyone's attention was focused on the Beatles at the time; Elvis was momentarily forgotten, and I sneaked in and pipped him.

But, nice as they all are, I'm afraid I haven't a clue now where most of the awards are. Some of them, I believe, are stacked away in packing-cases in the loft, some are at the office and, as I've mentioned, one or two have come in useful for odd functions about the house. But, apart from one time in Rookswood, when we actually had a Trophy Room and had to have special bars on all the windows to satisfy the insurance people, I've never bothered to keep tabs on them.

ABOVE One of those royal occasions – Madeleine Bell giggling away in the middle is one of the Prince's favourite artists.

BELOW Sharing a joke with Princess Alexandra, who presented our Music Therapy Award in '77 for 'outstanding services to the music industry'.

The important thing for me about an award is not the object itself but what it represents. And make no mistake that for me the biggest perk of them all is to know that people like what I do. Not everyone appreciates my music – I know that – but enough are sufficiently enthused to put records in the charts, pack concerts, and push TV shows up the ratings. I promise you, that's a most rewarding feeling and something I've never taken for granted.

This very week my latest single has made the Top Ten and I'm as excited now as when 'Move it' crashed in at the very start. OK, so I know a lot of it is plain old ego and that there are a thousand and one people who could be doing what I do a darn sight better if they had the opportunity. But, as I see it, in this instance ego isn't that far removed from job satisfaction. The craftsman achieves his through an item well-made, the salesman through satisfied customers, the businessman through increased profits – well, mine comes from a blend of the three – good performance, enthusiastic audiences, and successful business. Each one hinges on the other.

There's a verse in the New Testament that speaks volumes to me. It's something that Jesus said to His disciples when He was speaking generally about the things we have and enjoy. 'To whom much is given,' He said, 'much shall be required, for greater is their responsibility.'

ABOVE Elton John gives me the golden handshake for 'Devil Woman'.
BELOW Some of my most loyal and enthusiastic fans are in Japan.

11 A Way to Escape

PETER GORMLEY ONCE told me I was a very private person. He didn't mean it badly, in the sense of being unfriendly or anti-social, but rather that when I was 'off duty', so to speak, I tended to pull shutters down on the showbiz scene and most of the people in it. Thinking about it, I suppose he's right.

I do enjoy being at home, not doing anything in particular, just pottering around the garden maybe, walking the dog, or watching 'MacMillan & Wife' or 'Star Trek' on telly, and having Mamie thrust a bowl of cornflakes under my nose at the right moment. There's a kind of security about home that I can remember first sensing when I was a kid.

One of my favourite feelings was when there was a raging thunderstorm outside and I was in front of a warm fire on the inside. I'd have just had a bath and everything was clean and safe and untouched by all the violence going on around. I think my love of home is some kind of hangover from that and, even though I have no family ties, I get more homesick on tour than most of the musicians, who do. That's why these days I'm never away for more than three weeks on the trot. Invariably I'm counting the days after two!

Sometimes I do get guilty pangs at not making greater efforts to see showbiz friends socially. Quite a few of them live within about ten miles of home, some even less than that, so there's no real excuse.

It's the same with shows. I know that, from a purely professional point of view, I ought to visit the theatre much more than I do – maybe I'm not that dedicated. I prefer to rest on the fact that when I'm working I give myself wholly to the job. I demand a high standard from myself and everyone working with me. On stage I give all that I can and on every official public occasion I do my best to be available and approachable. In private though, Peter's right – the shutters are down.

In my public moments – by far the majority – I am very public; when I'm private I like it to stay that way! Fortunately I'm in a business where people are allowed their eccentricities.

For the do-it-yourself psychiatrists who'll now deduce that I'm a self-sufficient recluse or that deep down I'm really a very lonely guy, let me hasten to advise that you save your sympathy. I'm neither. Whilst I reckon I could enjoy living alone on the proverbial desert island for a while and be handyman enough to survive, my own company would wear thin before very long and I'd be all for getting back to people. It's the sort of people that's important.

I'm always hesitant to say I have a wide circle of friends because the meaning of 'friend' is so often devalued. If, by friends, you mean someone you like and who likes you on a fairly superficial level then, OK, it's a big circle. I'm surrounded professionally by people I like and who like what I do and who want my concert to be the best one in town, with the best sound and the best lighting. Now all that's very conducive to my being happy at my work and having good vibes with a lot of people, but it doesn't necessarily result in close personal friendships.

In that realm, the circle is a small one, limited to only a handful, and mostly to people outside show-business. I've never been one to treat relationships lightly and I object to people calling me a close friend when I'd barely even recognise them. I find that a total abuse and misuse of the word. When people knock at my front door or come to the theatre and spin a yarn about being a close friend, ninety-nine times out of a hundred I can be sure they're fake, and usually I'm blunt enough to say so. Maybe it's partly my fault, for I don't think I'm a difficult person to get to know.

I am fairly trusting, probably over-trusting, and I'm not a very good judge of character. I take people as I find them and, if they're pleasant to me, then I'm pleasant back but, as far as I'm concerned, that isn't friendship and I'm reluctant to throw the word around as easily as some people seem to.

I suppose bachelors are automatically regarded as lonely people and I've grown weary of the hoary old questions about marriage which usually have some built-in innuendo about homosexuality. Maybe it's our mixed-up society that's conditioned us to suspect that any adult who's single and over thirty must be sexually abnormal. Maybe it's just that we regard our public figures – particularly those who are depicted as 'whiter than white' – as legitimate Aunt Sallies – fair game to knock down and demolish, given the chance. Whatever the reason, I'm well aware that for years there's been speculation and rumour about why I've never married, and the only answer that I know and can give – that I've never been sufficiently in love with a girl nor she with me – apparently isn't good enough. Even if I were some shadowy homosexual, which I'm not, I'm hardly likely to say so, and any sexy skeletons that might be lurking in locked cupboards are going to stay put.

The fact is that Cliff Richard isn't whiter than white. At best he's a rather dirty grey. Certainly I've made mistakes, and still do, in all sorts of areas and in my own mind I'm acutely aware of failings and behaviour that I

Capital Radio's Kenny Everett has to be one of my favourite DJs.

OPPOSITE, ABOVE If this were colour, my face would be green! An hour's mackerel fishing with some friends off the Cornish coast was more than enough for me.

OPPOSITE, BELOW 'Don't do that!'

regret and which make me ashamed. But the media isn't a public confessional, and when I was converted God dealt with all that and eradicated it once and for all from the record. I for one have no intention of raking back through the past just to satisfy dubious curiosity, provide a new headline or even to scotch rumours. If people want to think the worst, I'm resigned to let them.

What I find mildly amusing is that my bachelorhood seems a much greater problem for other people than it is for me. I am content – I really am. Yet to listen to the probing, cautiously-phrased questions, and the spiritual advice I get from well-meaning Christians, you'd think I was undergoing some grave personal tragedy.

Do let's get things in proportion. Marriage is desirable. I've no doubt about that, and the idea of kids around the house appeals very much. But surely it isn't the be-all and end-all of living? For some, being single is part of God's plan, and there's little doubt that, if I had family and home commitments, a good chunk of what I do now and what I believe to be worthwhile would need radically pruning. On another level, sad reflection though it is, I'm actually the envy of some of my married friends whose homes aren't half as relaxed and happy as mine.

So, no, I don't have any great urge to be married. No, I'm not a mass of sexual hang-ups. Yes, I have had girlfriends in the past and, who knows, I may have another in the future and end up married. In the meantime, I'm not pursuing anyone and feel very fulfilled, thank you very much! Perhaps I'll give the next interviewer who starts the well-worn romance routine a copy of this book – it will save a lot of time and a lot of tedium.

One of the first things I do when I get home after a week or so away is inspect the garden. I'm no great gardener myself but love to see things grow and love just to enjoy a garden. By that, I mean pottering around, appreciating the beauty of it all. Some people I know are fanatical weeders and it beats me how anyone can really absorb a garden properly when their eyes are riveted the whole time on the two square feet just below them. It's as well we're all different! I wouldn't mind rushing round the place with a lawnmower, as long as it's got a motor and as long as Wally, our gardener, is standing by to do the edges!

Ours is an undulating lawn, packed with daisies in the summer, which always brings to mind the story of the radio Children's Hour scarecrow, Worzel Gummidge, who was asked to clear a lawn of daisies and make it look like a bowling green. 'I couldn't do that,' Worzel protested, 'the daisies are pinning the lawn to the ground.' But the woman insisted, the daisies were rooted out, and the lawn took off.

It's a nice idea and about as scatterbrained, I suppose, as the notion that plants respond to a friendly chat. But I did have a word with a droopy hibiscus once – when no one was around of course – and, whether it was that the sun filtered through a bit more strongly that week, I don't know, but the thing picked up and bloomed beautifully.

Botanically, my domain is really indoors. Half our rooms are like greenhouses and, although I'm not convinced about all that green-fingered stuff, I must admit they seem to thrive quite happily under my care. I'm well into all this cross-pollination business and, as soon as two blooms open simultaneously, I'm poking around with the paintbrush, giving nature a hand!

I feel I've been a bit of a help to her too by investing some money in trees. After hearing conservationists talk about the danger of increasing pollution from car exhausts and factory chimneys, and the possibility of an oxygen shortage, I asked my accountant to unravel some of the money that was tied up in Australian tin mines or whatever, and invest it instead in land.

Soon afterwards she 'phoned and told me about 500 wild acres in Snowdonia that the Forestry Commission were using to plant trees. It's a ridiculously long process of getting any return for your cash but the theory is that eventually you sell the wood and make a profit. We made the transaction and the last time I saw the trees they were literally six inches high and looked as though a stiff breeze would keel them over. What the 1976 drought did to them I've yet to discover!

But, despite the drawbacks, I felt rather pleased about doing my bit for posterity and, if I make it and Jesus doesn't come back first, I shall sit under my trees in Wales, breathing the oxygen they create and I paid for!

I hinted earlier that I'd make out quite well on a desert island. One thing for sure I wouldn't do is starve. Ask the kids who were on my boat on the Broads and they'll tell you about a shepherd's pie second to none. Nothing Cordon Bleu, you understand, and whether I'd be quite as enthusiastic if I had to concoct it every day is another thing, but give me a free hand in the kitchen and I'm in my element.

It seems to me that anyone who can read can cook – all you do is open a recipe book at the page that says 'Plum Duff' and read it and do it. The Plum Duff may not be as good as your mum makes but it's still a Plum Duff!

I went to my cottage in Wales for a week in the winter – just me, the dog, and my guitar. 'You'll be back by Tuesday,' they said at home. 'But take plenty of tins just in case.' OK, so I took the tins, but I lasted the week and put on three pounds!

If I were entering a culinary competition, I think I'd plump for the barbecue section. Although I say it myself, I'm rather a dab hand at barbecues, assuming I can get the thing alight. I try to prepare the steaks a day before, soaking them in wine and spices overnight. With some special spiced sausages from the local butcher, a Salad à la Richard, and a hunk of garlic bread, it has to be five-star quality. Maybe that's a possibility if ever I quit showbusiness – chef i/c barbecues – a bit seasonal, but then I could try my hand at waiting for the rest of the year. I've always thought I'd be good at that too!

Something else I enjoy at home is photography. It would be a bit presumptuous to say it was a hobby because serious photographers are into all the dark-room and the home-processing business, and that's too time-consuming for me. I just enjoy taking pictures and I've a cupboard bursting with arty close-ups of flower petals and sun glinting through trees.

Again I never have time to file them properly so if I want to show someone the shots of last year's holiday, it means a few hours of rummaging through dozens of identical boxes to find them.

I've had a couple of opportunities to show off my pictures – once when EMI used a portrait I took of my sister Donna on the back cover of the 'Kinda Latin' LP, and I reckon I was more proud of the tiny credit for that than for my name on the front.

The other time was when Kodak invited showbiz people to submit entries for what they called an 'Exhibition of the Stars'. They wanted two photographs and I couldn't make up my mind what to send; in the end I whittled down what I thought were passable to about twelve, and submitted the lot. To my genuine surprise and delight, they accepted eight of them, blew them up to a magnificent size, and hung them for public viewing for about a fortnight in a London gallery.

In any event, I prefer to be behind a lens rather than in front of it. Goodness knows how many photographers I've had to pose for to ensure those ever-current publicity shots but, unless the cameraman is a genius and can keep you talking and walking naturally, the exercise is generally a bore.

I found a good solution for a recent Palladium brochure – I took the pictures myself. If the neighbours had been peering through their rhododendrons, they'd have wondered what I was up to. The time exposure allowed me twelve seconds to hare seventy feet from pushing the button to the spot where I'd focused. I made it OK but instead of the dreamy and nonchalant pose I looked ready to drop after a four-minute mile! Still, they used two of the less puffed-looking ones and I guess no one was any the wiser.

One of the bonuses of living a couple of miles from the nearest bus-route is that fans find the trek a bit off-putting. It's the 'private person' rearing his head again no doubt, but I seldom go out of my way to give fans too warm a welcome at the front door. I'm not rude but they don't exactly get red-carpet treatment!

There's a small group of fans who are, in a way, special. They've been totally loyal through the years and we've built up a really good understanding. They're always courteous and thoughtful and usually come to the house twice a year, to say 'Happy birthday' and 'Happy Christmas'. That I appreciate. It's the demanding ones who are the drag – the ones who arrive at the house out of the blue and get stroppy if I'm not able to chat to them for half an hour. Usually they're the ones with a 'we made you so you owe us' attitude.

More excusable, but just as difficult, are the mentally disturbed ladies who turn up from time to time. One appeared on the doorstep recently with a couple of suitcases and announced she'd come to stay. She'd been 'told by the Lord', she said, that I needed her, so, at considerable personal expense, she was merely being obedient. I tried to get across that it was a bit surprising that the Lord hadn't told me about the arrangement too so that at least I could have prepared the spare room! It needed a couple of policemen to eventually get her and her ton-weight suitcases out of the house.

Then there was the girl who announced our forthcoming marriage in a local paper, and conned the vicar into reading the banns. I'd never set eyes on the girl before but I had a job convincing the vicar!

From a distance, it sounds funny; at close quarters, it's sad to encounter so many sick and lonely people – some of them long past the teenybopper age – and mighty embarrassing on occasions to be the object of their enacted fantasies.

I'm aware that a big bone of contention among a great many fans has been my reluctance to give the go-ahead for an official fan-club in Britain. There used to be one, a very efficient one at that, but it was wound up soon after my conversion when I had visions of a quick exit. Since then there have been several enthusiasts keen to get another organisation off the ground, and I've been asked many times to give my stamp of approval to this or that plan.

That's where it gets tricky for, as soon as the animal becomes 'official', I'm the one who really carries the can if things go wrong. If there are money problems or administrative difficulties, for instance, it would be my office staff who would have to come to the rescue. It's not that I don't appreciate the motives and, if people want to organise their own thing privately and without our endorsement, that's fine by me.

A long line-up for a signature at Selfridge's.

At the Highway Trust's centre for down-and-outs in
Plymouth. One of the few projects that Tear Fund
supports at home.

In fact there are a number of these unofficial clubs and one of the best of them is run from Holland. Although it goes under the impressive name of 'The International Cliff Richard Movement', it isn't the pseudo-commercial enterprise that so many of these things become. There's no pushing of glossy Cliff Richard pin-up posters or Cliff Richard tee-shirts, and kids are not tempted to part with their money for the latest promotional gimmick. It seems more of an appreciation society really, which provides information about me and my work schedule which isn't available through the press.

Another group, this time operating from Belgium, which I was particularly glad to see come together, was the 'Christian Friends of Cliff Richard'. Brainchild of a small group of Christian youngsters, the idea is to keep members informed primarily about my Christian commitments. At the same time, it spurs people to pray, provides an element of fellowship and encouragement and, most important, portrays what I do in a balanced and healthy perspective.

It's taken me quite a few years to accept the fact that fans can get converted too! Like the cynics, I tended to think that every time a fan expressed some interest in Christianity it was inevitably either fake or mindless 'follow-my-leader'. I'm aware still of both possibilities, let me add, and guess that if next year I took up with an obscure Peruvian sect which stood on one leg for five hours a day, there would be those sheeplike enough to follow. But that's only one side of it and discards the truth that God is as much concerned with the fan as He is with the star.

OK, so often there are ulterior motives but surely God is big enough and capable enough to work on bad motives and change them to good ones. It's probable that there are Christians reading this whose first move towards Christian things wasn't from the best of intentions. I think of Frank Morison, the author of the widely-read little booklet *Who Moved the Stone?* He approached the subject as an opponent, determined to disprove the resurrection account and reduce Christianity to a laughing-stock. That was his intention; God's intention was to show him the truth and, in the course of his research and discovery, Morison was converted.

I can think too of one girl who was an obsessive fan. Everywhere I went, she was there – outside studios, theatres, offices, home – everywhere. She wasn't a particularly pleasant girl and had a chip on her shoulder and a surly acid tongue. To cut a long story short, she followed me to churches, to evangelistic rallies and got converted. Today she's contributing to a missionary programme in South America. Occasionally I get a letter from her – she is happy, adjusted and fulfilled, and a reminder to me that what may start as misplaced Cliff Richard worship can be transformed and re-directed by the Holy Spirit into something worthwhile and productive.

Ironically, it's at my local church that I have most difficulty in remembering! I find it hard not to be irritated when I see fans dotted around the congregation – girls who I know full well wouldn't be there but for me. It's like them coming down the front path at home – an intrusion into an area that's important and private.

Probably I cope with it better at church than I do at home. I know I've got to accept it and, as one minister said, what's important is not *why* they come but *what we as a church do with them* once they're there. Obviously if those same girls in later months or years become an integral part of the church, regardless of whether I'm there or not, the personal irritation is immaterial!

I wonder how many people read the article in the Sunday paper that announced in large type that I'd quit the Church of England. It was another of those misleading half-truths which heralded the somewhat stale news that I'd been baptised. If readers were anticipating some dramatic row between the Anglican hierarchy and myself, it was anti-climax.

The simple and non-newsy fact was that when I moved my home from North London to Surrey I chose to attend a Baptist, instead of an Anglican, church because I found the teaching of one particular man helpful and stimulating.

I explained in an earlier chapter that I've never been a staunch denominational person. I'm honestly not too bothered whether I worship with Anglicans, Baptists, Methodists or Brethren, as long as Jesus is the focal point. In Surrey, as before, I needed to find a church where, on the comparatively few Sundays I was free, I could enjoy worship and be well taught. Fortunately, just twenty minutes away from home, there was a live, vibrant fellowship in which I immediately felt accepted and at home. As it happened, its label was Baptist.

Maybe, with hindsight, there's always been a bit of Baptist inclination in me because, even after my Anglican confirmation, I wasn't entirely satisfied that I'd met Scripture's requirements concerning baptism. Frankly, I don't believe that my infant christening meant a thing. It certainly didn't to me and, as I doubt if my parents thought much about it either, the whole exercise must have been little more than a superstitious ritual.

Confirmation was important because it symbolised a public stand, but it didn't satisfy a persistent little niggle which questioned whether spiritually I was still complete. Baptism seemed such an integral part of New Testament Christianity and I couldn't imagine a droplet of water dribbled on my head when I was a baby could be a proper substitute for that adult symbol of submission and obedience. It wasn't some inner heavy

ABOVE Arriving with Bill and the band for a
Tear Fund gospel concert in Jersey.

BELOW Introducing Tear Fund to the Speaker of the
House of Commons, the Rt. Hon. George Thomas.

theological conflict and I knew that, as far as I was concerned, baptism would have little significance in terms of a personal declaration of faith. I'd been declaring loudly for eleven years! It was literally just a feeling or a prompting – I needed and wanted to be baptised.

Very few people knew about the baptismal service. David Pawson, the pastor, knew of course; Bill was there to hold the towel; George and Pauline Hoffman, both Anglicans, wanted to share in it and were praying for me at their service; a Baptist minister friend and his family from Bournemouth were remembering me at theirs. Apart from that, no one knew and it must have been quite a surprise for the 600-strong congregation to see me suddenly stand up, take off my jacket and move forward.

Six others had been immersed before me but, although I'd been sitting near them, no one realised there was a seventh until I got up. For me, it was a fabulous, moving experience.

David Pawson had referred earlier to baptism symbolising a clean start and it was a strange feeling of lightness that I sensed as I clambered out of that little pool, all dripping and bedraggled. It wasn't anti-climax or emptiness but an acute awareness that I really was free of everything that spoilt and hindered and dragged me down. That's part of the fantastic miracle of what God does for a person.

Christianity isn't about living a life where hopefully, and with super will-power, you slowly get cleaner and cleaner until finally you're there as some snow-white angel. The Christian actually starts clean. Once we accept for ourselves all that Jesus offers and start heading in His direction, we're washed, rinsed, and hung out to dry right there and then and, I tell you, to be able to hold your head up high, knowing that as far as God is concerned there's not a single blot on your copybook is something to get enthused about.

Everyone's baptismal service is something special. Mine was beautiful, one of those spiritual 'highs' that come occasionally and which help you plough on through the 'lows'. In all, the service lasted over two hours and, after communion and David's final prayer, someone in the congregation shared a prophecy, words which he believed God was giving him spontaneously. Personally I haven't shared in what's called a 'charismatic' experience, although I do feel open to what the Lord has to give me, but that prophecy acted as a seal for me of God's presence at that service. Since then, I can't say that the quality of my Christian life has necessarily improved; what I do know is that I've done what I believe God wanted me to do and that little niggle about being incomplete is a thing of the past.

I still only get to my local church once, sometimes twice, a month.

Occasionally I'm asked to sing during a service or lead community singing before it starts. Usually, though, I get lost in the huge congregation and the anonymity of being one in a like-minded crowd is marvellous. That church, I think, is the only place where I can sit comfortably and enthralled for two and a half hours without so much as a wriggle or a glance at my watch.

It's after the service that I miss out a little, when the people I'd like to talk to hold back and the younger ones bring me crashing back to earth with questions about my hairdresser or my latest record. Still, I'd do exactly the same if I were in their place – or, on second thoughts, I'd never have plucked up the courage!

12 'I'll Never Be The Same Again'

MAYBE YOU WOULDN'T credit that seven days in Bangladesh could make a significant difference to a person's life – let alone to a seasoned traveller and to someone who spent his childhood in India to boot. Yet for once one of those extravagant press headlines was on target – ' "I'll never be the same again" says Cliff'. It's what I actually said when I returned and, with a few years' hindsight, I believe I was right. But, as they say in storybooks, I must start at the beginning and tell you about Tear Fund.

Tear Fund crept into my life just when I needed it. It's an odd thing to say about a relief agency but that's the way it was – another of those 'timely accidents'. Tear Fund didn't latch on to me for a bandwagon promotion or a source of income. That's not their approach. I latched on to them because, as a young Christian, I wanted very much to be useful.

For sure, I was doing the rounds of meetings and church services but I knew that stewardship involved more than time. I had a high earning capacity and a talent, and that had to be channelled somehow in God's direction. But how to know what was right for me? That was the problem. I was determined not to throw money into a void or some kind of anonymous pool and, to be honest, I had no particular burden for any charity, either in Britain or overseas.

It was David Winter who first suggested Tear Fund. David was editor of *Crusade* magazine at the time and its parent organisation, the Evangelical Alliance, had apparently given birth to a new and very lively youngster. Its full title was The Evangelical Alliance Relief Fund. Conveniently, the initials made it Tear Fund!

Its business was to channel gifts from Christians in Britain to enable Christians in needy places around the world to get stuck into relief and development work. In most cases, that meant coming alongside missionaries involved maybe in preventive medical programmes or agricultural training. Sometimes it meant helping nationals, possibly mobilised to bring relief after an earthquake or flood. The point was that it was aid given always in the context of an evangelical Christian witness – and that appealed.

My first visit to Bangladesh had a profound effect upon me.

The concept of Christ being concerned about needs of 'whole' people was clear enough in Scripture but somehow it had never registered forcefully before. About that time I attended the European Conference on Evangelism in Amsterdam and remember hearing Gilbert Kirby, the Principal of London Bible College, saying that it was time that evangelical Christians stopped talking about saving people's souls and referred instead to saving people.

To a large extent, my early involvement with Tear Fund was self-centred. It was to give me a sense of satisfaction and fulfilment and I don't pretend I felt any heartache for the people in the Third World, or anywhere else, come to that. In retrospect, I don't think that was so very wrong. We've all got to start somewhere and I know that the lack of concern wasn't because of any calculated decision not to care – it was because I didn't really know. And I didn't know because I'd never made the effort to find out.

The progression since has been inevitable. When I got involved with Tear Fund I began to learn; when I learned I got enthused; and enthusiasm invariably leads to commitment. Today that commitment to Tear Fund and its 'love in action' philosophy is very deep indeed and the annual series of gospel concerts we present around the country to raise funds and to present Jesus is one of the high spots of my year.

The embryo of those concerts happened at the Albert Hall in London in 1968. David Winter devised the theme of 'Help, Hope and Hallelujah' and it was the first time I appeared on a concert platform without a repertoire and a backing group of old faithfuls. No 'Living Doll' or 'Lucky Lips', no Hank Marvin, Bruce Welch or familiar session musicians. In their place were numbers like 'It is no secret' and 'What a Friend we have in Jesus', and on stage with me were the Settlers folk group.

In more ways than one, it was quite a landmark. The concert was fabulous: we raised over £2,000 to enable an ambulance to go to South America and, for the first time, I was launched into the Tear Fund orbit. Just a little later, and quite independently, Tear Fund's Director, George Hoffman, personally invited Bill Latham to share the growing load of administration. Bill agreed, left the classroom and became Tear Fund's first Education Secretary and later its Deputy Director. For me, the writing was on the wall.

I guess that at least ninety per cent of Tear Fund's income is from people who have never been and who are never likely to go to the Third World. Africa or Asia or South America are about as remote as the moon. The aftermath of an earthquake or the misery of a malnourished child can only be imagined with the help of news reports, photographs and relief agency posters. Yet for many that's enough to prompt caring and giving, and thank God that it is so.

At the other extreme, there's a compassion born from experience and at that level I doubt if anyone brought up in the West can make the grade. Who of us, for instance, can really identify with a mother who has lost ten of her twelve children through tetanus or starvation? What do we know of the despair of a father whose subsistence crop has been wiped out by flood or blight? We can try to understand but sharing that kind of burden is well-nigh impossible.

I'm not very bright at drawing theological parallels but that does tell me something about the mystery of God becoming man. It wasn't enough for God to imagine our problems and anxieties; it wasn't sufficient even for Him to come and watch them; complete understanding and perfect love meant experiencing the whole gamut of pain and deprivation for Himself. That's what I understand the Cross to be about. Because of what happened there, I can never say – and I don't believe you can ever say – 'Lord, you don't understand', because He always does – He's been through it.

In between those two extremes of caring, there's 'seeing for oneself'. Not imagining, not experiencing, but first-hand watching. In one sense, it's the easiest and privileged route to caring; in another, it's the most disturbing. I have this daft notion that everyone should be compelled to spend time in an area of real poverty. A fortnight would do. There would be a mass shift of values, I guarantee.

My opportunity to see first-hand came *en route* home from Australia. I had been performing at the Sydney Opera House a few days after its official opening. At the same time, George Hoffman and Bill Latham were in Bangladesh, visiting Tear Fund projects, and I was invited to tag along. It would be an ideal chance to make a soundstrip and, according to Bill, it would be 'valuable experience'. I'd no idea just how valuable and I don't think he had either!

Flying into Dacca, the Bangladesh capital, via Dum Dum Airport, Calcutta for the first time, guarantees at least mild culture shock for anyone from the West. Coming straight from the extravagance of the Opera House, with the popping of champagne corks still loud in the ears, meant a degree of mental and emotional adjustment I couldn't cope with.

In Australia I'd been impressed by one of man's most spectacular creative achievements; in Bangladesh I watched an eighteen-month-old baby die of starvation because its parents couldn't afford to feed it. In Australia I left behind my stage suits and smart gear and kept with me a toothbrush, spare pair of jeans and a guitar: just that was enough to put me in a class apart. People in Bangladesh don't have spare anything. A nurse told me that when a patient is admitted to hospital he enters into the ward just as he is; there's nothing at home to fetch.

On the first day I remember wandering, almost in a daze, around one of the Bihari refugee camps. Liz, one of the nurses Tear Fund was supporting, said she wouldn't take us into the worst as we'd need Wellington boots to walk through the sewage. After what seemed hours of looking and looking away, I asked George about lunch. I wasn't hungry but I'd had enough. George said something about 'funny eating habits' and told me it was only ten a.m. – we'd been out barely a couple of hours.

That first morning I must have washed my hands a dozen times. Whenever we stopped, I made a beeline for the communal tap or the well; I didn't want to touch anything, least of all the people. Everyone in those camps, even the babies, was covered in sores and scabs.

I was bending down to one little mite, mainly for the photographer's benefit, and trying hard not to have too close a contact, when someone accidentally stood on the child's fingers. He screamed out and, as a reflex, I grabbed hold of him, forgetting all about his dirt and his sores. I remember now that warm little body clinging to me and the crying instantly stopped. In that moment I knew I had an enormous amount to learn about practical Christian loving but that at least I'd started.

I understood too from that little incident how starved those kids were of affection. Parents hadn't the strength or the inclination to show it; survival was too exhausting. I didn't know it at the time but George took a picture of me standing ashen-faced with that little boy buried in my shoulder; today a huge enlargement of that snap is one of my most treasured and meaningful possessions. It hangs on the wall between my bedroom and bathroom, where I can't fail to see it or remember it.

The press didn't get wind of my time in Bangladesh until about a year later. When they did print an article, with some predictably slanted and misleading headline, I received a lot of mail from people who were under the impression that I'd done something heroic and sacrificial simply because I'd been there. In fact it was no such thing. For a start, I stayed at the five-star Intercontinental, and that relates to the reality of Bangladesh about as much as Dr Who's time machine to some prehistoric culture.

In the Intercontinental there are iced drinks, clean sheets and air-conditioning; beggars are kept at a discreet distance, and a man in a peaked cap, who holds the door open, has you believing that it's your lifestyle that's normal and everyone else is out of step.

Maybe it was a necessary breaking-in – I don't know; possibly I would have wilted if there were no escape at all from the stench and the suffering and the degradation of it all. But personally the only hardship was to feel so absolutely wretched and helpless in the face of it.

Each night, we used to meet with the nurses in their home; we'd sing a bit, George would comment on some Bible verses, and everyone would be very open and frank. I remember saying to someone that it seemed almost a cheat that I should go back to England and continue to be Cliff Richard – it was all so easy. I would go ahead and do my twenty concerts for Tear Fund and raise £25,000 and I'd enjoy every minute of it. Compared to what others were contributing it seemed so puny.

I see now that that was illogical but it took one of the girls to help me realise it. 'Without you and other Christians at home,' she said, 'we wouldn't be here! We need each other.' That was a real consolation at the time and the words stuck. I reckon we often fall into the trap of surrounding missionaries with a kind of glamour and slot them into a Division One spiritual league; they're the people, we think, out on a limb for Christ; they're the ones who are really testing the power of God every day, and the rest of us are fiddling around having it all so cushy.

What I learned, I suppose, was another dimension of Paul's 'body' illustration – that each of us has a different function which, in its own way, is as crucial as the other. What use would I be in Bangladesh, for instance? I'm not qualified to do anything that would help towards progress. Maybe I could sweep up or hump stuff around a hospital but anyone could do that, and a Bengali needs the job more. The fact is that God moves some of us around and others He uses where they are. I reckon – at the moment, at least – that I have to take up my role right here and, if I'm not out on a limb for Christ just as much as I theoretically might be in Bangladesh, then there's something wrong.

Some of my most vivid memories of Bangladesh are very positive – like the patient who was so proud of a bullet embedded in his side that he insisted that everybody should feel it. He developed a fascinating party trick of rolling the bullet around under his skin and thought he was really going to lose out if surgeons had their way and removed it!

Then there was the marvellous atmosphere in the children's ward in Dacca's one and only barn of a hospital. Many of the kids were dreadfully injured, sick or burned, yet the happiness in that place was a tonic and, as I say on the narrative of Tear Fund's filmstrip which we called 'Love never gives up', I'm sure that that happiness was a reflection of the love and care shown by Tear Fund's nurses there.

One has to understand too that in Bangladesh the fact of having an arm missing, or even part of your face blown away, isn't the socially damaging thing it would be to us. For the average Bengali, as for most people struggling to live in developing countries, it doesn't matter a scrap how you look or how you dress – what matters is whether you can function sufficiently to survive. If you've got a stump for an arm, for instance, the vital factor is whether you're able to move it and put it to use.

I've heard George and Bill say many times that one of their reasons for optimism, despite the vastness of the problems, is the evidence of God's love in action. I wasn't sure what they meant before Bangladesh; I hoped it wasn't just spiritual jargon. Having spent those few days with a bunch of nurses out for a year or two, and a few 'lifetime' missionaries – although I doubt whether the distinction is very relevant these days – I know what they meant.

Here were people putting into practice a depth of compassion that was communicating to government officials, community leaders, expatriates and patients alike. Through their actions they were earning the right to speak and, while many others involved in relief work were wringing their hands in despair and frustration, these ambassadors of Jesus were reflecting a quality almost extinct in Bangladesh – hope.

When you think about it, it makes absolute sense. If you're not a Christian, what do you offer these people, other than bread? There may come a day when even the bread stops and what do you do or say then? Christian help goes so much deeper. Instead of a 'three score and ten' perspective, the Christian thinks in terms of eternity, and that's where the hope lies.

People often ask whether my faith in a God of love was shaken by Bangladesh. In fact it was the contrary. Soon after arriving in Bangladesh, one of Tear Fund's nurses asked Hester Quirk, the senior missionary, how she could be sure there was a God of love, in view of all the suffering. 'I know,' said Hester, 'because He sent you here.'

And that's it – God unmistakably at work, as He always has been, through His people. Of course there's no way that I can begin to understand *why* the suffering but, brought down to a personal family level, it's always troubled me that one of the first questions we ask after a sudden death or an accident is 'Why did God allow it to happen?' It's incredible how people who never think of God any other time blame Him when there's a tragedy. No one ever thinks of asking 'Why the devil . . .?' Personally I believe that it's Satan who's responsible for much of the world's suffering – and man who's responsible for the rest. Satan's ploy backfires when men of totally different culture and religion ask to hear more about God and Jesus as a result of Christians caring.

Humanly speaking, it's so easy too to retreat and convince ourselves that

ABOVE Everywhere we went in Bangladesh there were children. This is one of the Bihari refugee camps with Tear Fund's Director, George Hoffman, and former Deputy Director Bill Latham.

BELOW It was an emotional experience to sing in Mother Theresa's Home for the Destitute and Dying in Calcutta.

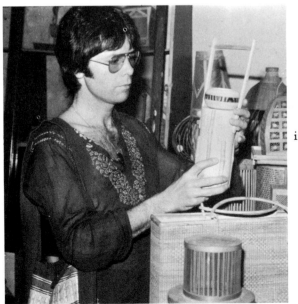

TOP With Mother Theresa and her Sisters of Charity in Calcutta. I've never met a more Jesus-centred person.

CENTRE When you meet Mother Theresa, it helps to understand Jesus a little better.

LEFT One way of helping the developing world is to purchase its handicrafts.

it's all so futile. 'So,' we argue, 'Tear Fund supports forty people in Bangladesh – what's that among eighty million? A tiny drop in a vast bucket.' Drop it may be, but at least the bucket's moist. Something is happening; somebody is being helped.

We tend to get bogged down with statistics and comparisons and think only in terms of millions. Yet surely if one starving person came to your front door, you'd feed him, and that's something really positive – one person, a human being, has actually been helped! But in Bangladesh we're not talking about just one person; we're talking of thousands.

It seems we have two choices – either we go ahead and help a bit or we say it's hopeless and do nothing. On second thoughts, the Christian has no choice. Regardless of how physically hopeless a situation may appear, we have to do what God would have us do and our contribution is going to be connected with some living being who's made in God's image and who is going to be helped and affected. In no way is that futile!

I can't see that I'm ever going to forget what I learned in Bangladesh. I think I said to a press man that I returned a different person. On reflection, I think that was a bit over-dramatic. After all, how many times can a person change? When I became a Christian, I certainly changed then. Bangladesh though was more of a growing-up experience and I doubt if God gives that kind of lesson to people to have it wear off after a few years. Whoever heard of growing down?

Nepal and Southern Sudan, two other countries I visited wearing a Tear Fund hat, were much less harrowing experiences, although travelling 300 miles with a slipped disc in a Land-Rover over bush tracks in Sudan wasn't an experience I'd recommend! If any roads existed before the civil war between north and south, there was certainly no trace left afterwards. It was a bone-shattering journey.

After a few hours, our petrol tank was holed and one facility you won't find in the depths of the Sudanese jungle is a garage. Alarmingly, Alfred, our African driver, disappeared without a word into the bush, leaving a crowd of half-naked tribesmen jostling to fill up their cigarette lighters under the leak. Half an hour and a few prayers later, Alfred reappeared with a lump of soap and a wadge of cotton-wool. I hadn't a clue what use they were but I admired his resourcefulness. Admiration grew to a kind of awed respect as he rubbed the soap into the cotton to form a brilliantly effective plug. Not another drop was spilled from that tank and, to my knowledge, it's still holding together!

The problems of Sudan are a huge contrast to those of Bangladesh. Instead of a densely crowded population, desperate for emergency help, the five million Southern Sudanese are needing long-term aid – help to pick up the threads of community living again after seventeen years of bitter fighting.

Nothing survived the war – no schools, hospitals, communications, houses or factories – everything had to start from scratch, and again Tear Fund was supporting personnel in an important rural development programme. Here people were being helped to help themselves, to plant the right crops at the right time, to administer their own medicines, to observe certain principles of hygiene, and to use their latent skills in handicrafts and building.

Medically, as I say, the emphasis was on training and prevention and I remember watching boggle-eyed in a tiny bush clinic as a nurse cut a tiny piece of skin from a man's leg to test against river-blindness. Apparently this disease, a scourge in many parts of Africa, is caused by a fly which lays its eggs just below the surface of the skin. The worms are comparatively harmless until they inch their way towards the eyes. Once they're in the optic region, blindness is inevitable and incurable.

Through a course of injections, the bugs can be expelled from the body before they reach the danger zone. I have a shrewd suspicion that the nurse, an Australian lady with a wicked sense of humour, revelled in having a squeamish Pommy around the place for a day. Certainly she took delight in showing me the piece of skin under her microscope to prove her point about wriggly worms!

By the time we'd travelled our 300 miles to a place called Rumbek, with two or three off-beat overnight stops *en route*, the back was definitely dodgy. Imagine how I felt when I learned that I was to give an open-air concert that very evening to the schoolkids of the area. No microphones, no amplification – just me, an acoustic guitar, two or three hundred kids, and a handful of bemused village chiefs. It was no use arguing – word had gone out on the bush telegraph and that was that.

The missionary guy, an American, hadn't quite realised that anyone more than about five yards away wouldn't hear a sound. Maybe he thought I was an operatic tenor.

There were probably nearer five hundred in the audience in the end. Most had never heard of Cliff Richard and probably concluded I was a mime artist. They were very polite though and I did most of my repertoire walking up and down the rows like a restaurant minstrel. The whole thing was a hoot – once it was over! What Peter Gormley would say I can't imagine.

If that wasn't indignity enough, I crowned it by being sick on the flight back. It was one of those little 'planes, bumped all over the place by turbulence, and I was stretched out at the back, trying to get my back comfortable. But to get off a 'plane, be it a Jumbo or a six-seater, clutching your own sick-bag, doesn't do much for your star status!

Despite the real affinity I have with Tear Fund, I was in two minds about accepting their invitation to sit on the Main Council. In one sense I was chuffed to think they regarded me as Council calibre, but in another I was very conscious of my own limitations and know full well that I'm no committee man. However, I accepted and I sat through the first couple of meetings with a dozen or so high-powered experts, feeling I ought to contribute something but aware that I had nothing really to offer in discussion about development policy or administrative procedures.

More recently I've come to terms with that particular problem and recognise that the value of my Council membership lies not in what I can inject but rather in what I can take away and share with others via interviews and meetings.

So many people have said that they have gained much more from involvement with Tear Fund than they have contributed to it. Undoubtedly that's true in my case. Anything I may have learned about myself and other people, about materialism and priorities, about suffering, about people who quietly go away to places like Bangladesh and Sudan and do their thing for Jesus – all that and much more has come about directly because of links with Tear Fund. Unreservedly I commend it to your prayers and to your support.

13 For Art's Sake

I KNOW MANY people in show-business who do a great deal of tremendous work for charities yet who have no personal commitment to any of them. That's not criticism. If your policy is to spread the net wide and earmark time for a hundred and one different charities during the course of a year, then there's no alternative. Once you've opened the fête, drawn a raffle or done your act, you can hardly be expected to keep up a practical interest for ever after.

Personally, I prefer to spend more time with a few rather than a little time with many. In that way I'm able to be more involved and believe, rightly or wrongly, that I can be of more use. There are a few 'one-offs', all the same – like SOS, the Stars' Organisation for Spastics. I'm often asked to take part in one of their fund-raising efforts and, although as part of the business I feel morally obliged to lend my weight now and again, I don't honestly feel 'into it' as I would, say, with a Tear Fund effort.

PHAB, which stands for Physically Handicapped and Able Bodied and is a branch of the National Association of Youth Clubs, attracted my attention a long while back. I'm what might be called 'sleeping president' but wake up every so often to meet a bunch of members, maybe at a theatre or a training course.

The idea behind PHAB is simply to break down some of those barriers which make communication between physically handicapped and able-bodied people uneasy and embarrassing. Its aim really is to help under-standing – not only so that the fit and well can be more at ease with the handicapped, but vice versa. The concept is great, and some of the old hang-ups I used to have when talking with spastic kids or even blind people have disappeared, in large measure due to PHAB's practical common-sense.

There was the time, for instance, at the PHAB disco. I had the shock of my life to discover that modern music is tailor-made for spastics. Suddenly the jerky movements and lack of co-ordination all absolutely fitted and, as I pranced around the floor with my spastic partner, anyone watching would have been hard put to tell which one of us was disabled!

Really though, there's only one other organisation, in addition to Tear Fund, that I'm involved in deeply and personally, and that's the Christian Arts Centre. Probably you've never heard of it. Unlike Tear Fund, it's a 'closed shop' affair, with a ministry aimed only at those people who earn their living in the arts world – and that includes just about every facet of art you can think of – showbiz, painting, writing, music, dancing, the whole spectrum. Whereas its work is confined to a comparative handful of people however, I've a feeling in my bones that, given time, the ripples from the Arts Centre are going to influence a much, much wider public.

It all started in the establishment setting of my Anglican church in Finchley in North London. Nigel Goodwin, a Christian actor, was speaking to the youth fellowship and in those days I was considered eligible to sit in! Nigel is one of those open friendly people you get to know very quickly and, obviously, as we were in much the same line of business, we had plenty of common ground right from the start.

Over a cup of coffee later in the evening, at David Winter's place, Nigel told us about his vision, still a bit blurred then, but vision I'm sure it was, of some kind of pad where Christians in the arts could come and talk and discuss and share their problems. Nigel is a tremendously gentle, caring person and his great burden then was, and I guess still is, the vast chasm that existed between the church and the arts.

The church, on the one hand, had written off the arts as beyond the pale; the arts, on the other, dismissed the church as irrelevant and pathetic. Somehow there had to be some bridge-building. That's about as far as we got on that occasion but it was far enough to sow a few seeds in my mind. I was impressed by Nigel's warmth and enthusiasm, and agreed a hundred per cent with his thinking.

Within a few months we'd met again, focused our plans more clearly, and formed a small unofficial committee. Then followed what seemed like donkeys' years – in fact it was only a couple – of thinking and talking and praying, and driving about London looking for a property, fairly central and comparatively cheap, that could be used as a base.

At the back of our minds too we were thinking about a second place, bigger and out in the country, which would be ideal for busy artists to visit, maybe for a weekend, to relax and unwind and discover that they weren't so much out on a limb in their jobs as they imagined. What we didn't expect was to find the country house before sorting out London. Nevertheless, that's the way it was.

Battailles, a beautiful house near Great Dunmow in Essex, with eleven acres of land, a squash court, stables, and about eight bedrooms, came on the market and I was in a position to buy it. Immediately after the deal was buttoned up, a property appeared for a ludicrously low rent in London, perfectly situated a few yards off Kensington High Street. All of a sudden, the Arts Centre was in action on two fronts, admittedly groping a bit in the

early days, but launched with the absolute conviction that God was in it and for it.

A dual operation, with Nigel and Gillian Goodwin in charge in London, and Jack and Pauline Filby running Battailles, worked well enough for a bit. I've heard of many people who found at Battailles a real help and encouragement. But, with hindsight, it was a mistake. We wanted to run before we could walk and the running costs of Battailles were beyond us. Regretfully, the country pad had to go and we said farewell to the Filbys.

Since then things have snowballed at Kensington. Various groups have come together under the Arts Centre umbrella – LEAP for the dancers, ACTS – surprise, surprise – for actors, MABEL (don't ask me why) for musicians, and groups too for broadcasters, graphic designers, journalists and painters. Rarely a week goes by without some special event to challenge and absorb at least one of the categories. Professor Rookmaaker from Holland, for instance, has been a guest speaker on several occasions and his wise advice, backing, and enthusiasm have been a big encouragement, particularly to Nigel.

Whilst it's not necessarily the church's fault, it's a fact that many Christians in the arts find difficulty in achieving any worthwhile or satisfying relationship with the church. Generally, Christian leaders, both at national and local level, don't understand painting or dancing or acting and, even less, the motivation that prompts the artist to follow his craft. Badly needed are front-line Christians, preferably with some first-hand personal experience in the arts, who understand artistic pressures and temperaments and can relate them to Scripture.

Our own ideas of course have crystallised a good deal as the work has grown. In terms of evangelism, for instance, we were very unsure at the start just what our responsibility was. We knew, if we grabbed people by the shoulder and asked whether they were saved, we might as well forget the whole idea. Yet at the same time we realised that part of the aim at least was to increase the Christian influence within the arts world, and that meant increasing the number of Christians!

Currently the arts world generally is pretty pagan, and what's coming out of the showbiz scene in particular makes a great many people sick. The problem is that the public get what they deserve or, more to the point, what they'll pay for! If they support rubbish, that's what they'll be given. If film-makers know that millions will queue to see a sex orgy, then artistic integrity goes to the wall and sex orgies will be churned out till they cease to be box office.

Sad though it is, the principal consideration of the film industry is to make money and if the public honestly wants clean entertainment it will

ABOVE One of the first bases for the Christian Arts Centre was Battailles, a fabulous house near Dunmow in Essex.

BELOW Larry Norman is a gifted gospel song-writer whose material I often use.

have to put its cash where its mouth is and make the effort to support those who give it.

In many ways I admire Mary Whitehouse enormously. Most of the time I agree with her arguments and her protests, but not always with the way she expresses them. But Mary is a lady at least ten years ahead of her time. In the 'sixties, she was warning our society about impending moral landslides and everyone laughed and scoffed and drew cartoons. But it's happened and, if anyone doubts it, let him cast his eye down the entertainments' column of a London newspaper!

I don't pretend to know what the answer is now we've got the rubbish but the Arts Centre are tackling it in their way and Mary in hers. And, as far as I'm concerned, all power to her!

One notion I want to dispel about the Arts Centre is that it's made up of a bunch of people who paint religious pictures and sing nothing but gospel songs. Not so, and this is where I'm likely to part company with quite a few Christians.

It's my conviction that a Christian artist's work becomes Christian simply because it must inevitably reflect the person responsible. What I mean is that, if a Christian painter paints a landscape, it will automatically be a Christian view of that landscape and therefore a Christian painting. It doesn't have to depict the Last Supper or the Crucifixion or Mary and Child.

Similarly, a singer, when he's converted, doesn't suddenly have to limit his repertoire to songs that mention Jesus. Why should he? In this sense, every pop song I perform becomes a Christian song because you can't divorce me from it. When I released 'Devil Woman' there were a number of Christians who took me to task for singing what they assumed were witchcraft lyrics. What those Christians had failed to do was, firstly and inexcusably to my mind, listen to the whole lyric, which is very clearly a warning *not* to get involved in that scene; secondly, I believe most were 'conditioned' into a non-Christian interpretation rather than a Christian one.

This whole dichotomy between secular and spiritual is a fascinating subject. As Christians we have to be involved in life and the very essence of artistic skill is to reflect life. In the course of that reflection, it may be necessary for an actor to play an ugly non-Christian role in order to highlight the contrast between good and bad, moral and immoral. But surely we don't slam him for that or question his spiritual integrity.

In my own situation again, pop lyrics – even a trite little love song – are, to my mind a valid reflection of very real aspects of life. Now I hope I'm not sounding pretentious – all that high-falutin' waffle that's spouted by the 'heavy brigade' of pop leaves me cold and the last thing I want is to sound like them. I'm not suggesting, of course, that pop has any hidden spiritual depths or that there's really no difference between my secular and gospel concerts. Of course there's a distinction but it's not the one you might think. In a nutshell, it's that an audience at a pop show watches a Christian entertaining; at a gospel concert they hear him evangelising. Although I've heard a good many Christians coming out of my pop concerts glad to have been entertained by a Christian, I don't know of anyone who's been converted at one! To me, you see, that's a real and important distinction, and yet there's no conflict. We're not creatures of continual work and slavery; occasionally we must smile and laugh, clap and tap our feet. Under whose influence and leadership do we do it? That's the point.

Gradually I sense the old strait-laced view of people in the arts world being all immoral and unprincipled layabouts is changing and it's up to the Arts Centre and groups like it to help speed things up. Steve Turner and Norman Stone, poet and film-maker respectively, are the kind of guys who'll be the catalysts. To an extent, they already are.

Steve's book of poetry, *Tonight we will fake love,* has already received wide acclaim by the critics, and Norman Stone has made his mark with a film allocated prime TV time. Both are young artists; both, I'm proud to say, have close ties with the Arts Centre and are committed Christians; and both, I've no doubt, are going to wield significant influence through the media.

The implications are exciting and it's even more so to realise there are dozens of other budding Turners and Stones within the Arts Centre ranks. They're not today's star names (although two or three of those are around as well) but beginners and students – names that will be famous tomorrow, people who have a talent and who are going to use it in a cynical and apathetic arena because they believe that's where God wants them.

As I say, there are just a few household names on the Arts Centre's membership list and in the early days we were disappointed there weren't more. I suppose we imagined getting through to a superstar category and seeing the likes of Sir Laurence Olivier, Rudolph Nureyev and Tom Jones getting converted and turning the whole showbiz scene upside-down overnight – that would have been glamorous and spectacular but it wasn't God's way, and we see now a much wiser long-term strategy.

It's strange, but once we'd realised that and accepted it, God seemed to give opportunities to reach these more senior, established people. A series of late-night suppers in Kensington, with just a handful of specially-invited celebrity guests, who we knew would be basically sympathetic, have resulted in some fabulous chats and hopefully paved the way for further contact. Roy Castle and his wife, Fiona, for instance, became actively involved once they heard what we were all about and realised the thing wasn't being run by a bunch of star-struck cranks – and that hurdle in itself takes some straddling.

People in the public eye are wary of ulterior motives; they don't want to be gawped at in public meetings, or feel that any tentative move towards spiritual things will result in daft comment in the press the following day. That's why the Arts Centre environment is ideal: there's no public, individuals can be themselves, the atmosphere is easy and relaxed, the Bible study isn't an embarrassing showing-up of what we don't know but an honest attempt to learn.

Hopefully the suppers, the midweek meetings and the fellowship won't be regarded permanently as an alternative to church. Initially they might be that and I can understand it, but the Arts Centre is no 'membership only' church, like some exclusive golf club. Rather we see it as a stepping-stone, a gentle breaking-in that will eventually give even the famous the confidence and inclination to join the wider family of God's people. If the family gawps – and Christians are no less impressed by a TV face than anyone else – then the Arts Centre may have laid a foundation that will bear it.

Like every effective Christian ministry, the Arts Centre has an army of prayer supporters. Five hundred people, most of them nothing to do with the arts world, but who are committed to the Arts Centre principle, have undertaken to pray regularly for it. Many of them contribute financially as well, even though they're not eligible for membership. Five hundred is good, but a thousand would be better.

Raising money for the Arts Centre is really a struggle. Understandably, there isn't the immediate obvious benefit that there is in a Tear Fund appeal, neither does the Arts Centre have a ministry which, in the short term, directly affects very many people. Added to that, there's the fallacy that everyone in the arts world is rolling in money, and the assumption that 'if Cliff Richard is involved then they must be well off!'

The Arts Centre isn't well off and may I say with respect that if some of those well-intentioned people who are quick to shriek their protests and write to newspapers about the latest blue movie were as agile with their wallets, I suspect that a great deal more positive good could be achieved.

That leads me to one last plea for understanding. Please, Christians, we need your encouragement, your prayers and your love, not your apathy or your antagonism. The fact that today there are many Christians working professionally within the arts world, maintaining a consistent witness and knowing the reason for the hope that is in them, is destroying the myth that Christian discipleship and public entertainment are irreconcilable.

In the words of Larry Norman – or was it General William Booth – 'Why should the devil have all the good music?'

14 Only Human

IF I HAD three wishes, I think I'd use them all up on a triple-layered skin! It would be so nice to go through life absolutely immune to criticism and mud-slinging. After nearly twenty years in the so-called 'public eye', I've never got used to it and, although I've virtually perfected a 'couldn't-care-less' façade, a vicious press write-up still gives me sleepless nights.

Most performers – most people, come to that – are the same. We like to be liked. Even the strongest, most self-sufficient character must get the tiniest bit upset when he's misunderstood, portrayed as a half-wit, and his work is torn to shreds by some biased critic. I've still got a long way to go in coping with criticism, whether it's professional and public, or private and poisonous.

Now I know full well that if I don't like it I can get out and retire to some quiet backwater. I know that I'm ultra-sensitive and that's another fault I have to cope with. I'm aware too that over the years the press have treated me very generously and, although I don't believe for a minute the nonsense about any publicity being good publicity, the column space they've allocated to me must run into a good few miles. The problem is that every now and then a newspaper will print something so distorted, misleading and offensive that years of good press relationships are demolished in a few paragraphs.

I'm proud of my reputation for being thoroughly professional. I think it's a justified reputation: I expect the best from myself and from the people around me. If they're not prepared to give it, then the answer is simple – they don't work with me. Tatty standards irritate me, and journalism is no exception.

In my view, journalists who twist truth are unprofessional and should be kicked out of their jobs. They're like bad dancers, bad actors, bad musicians – they ought not to be there. The arts world, more than any other, needs sensitive people who have principles, standards, and some sense of moral responsibility.

Let me tell you about two recent press articles and you can judge for yourself. One was in the *Daily Mail* and sparked off the fiasco concerning the 'Honky Tonk Angel' record.

If ever there was a mountain made of a molehill, it was this. Contrary to what some people suspected, I actually had no idea that a honky tonk was American slang for a bar prostitute. Naïve it may have been, but I didn't know. Nor did most of the people around me at the time. To me it was, and still is, a lovely country-and-western ballad with innocuous lyrics.

However, before long it was apparent that certain Christians in Britain thought otherwise and were more informed about Americans worldly jargon than I was! When a very sweet girl asked me at a student meeting how, as a Christian, I could release a record about a prostitute, I decided it was best to let the record die a quiet death. I still didn't personally see anything wrong with the lyric, even in the light of my new education, but clearly it was going to offend some people and I took the view that there was enough aggro around without adding more. So, as I say, I thought I'd not go out of my way to promote the song and it would come and go with minimum fuss.

That's what I thought and that's why I told Russell Harty on one of his TV chat shows that, instead of singing my latest single, I'd prefer to do one of my own compositions. That was OK by Russell but apparently not for a columnist of the *Daily Mail*, who must have overheard the conversation.

The next morning an inside-page headline declared 'Cliff wants his happy hooker disc banned'. What followed was three-quarters of a column, with quotes ascribed to me that were total invention: 'I have asked my record company to withdraw it', I was supposed to have said. 'I'm going to have the BBC take it off the play-list.' And so on and so on. Now, apart from the fact that those were the last things I intended doing, I didn't give any kind of interview to the reporter, although I remember he was very insistent that I should give him five minutes.

What alarms me is that his 'professionalism' – or lack or it – permitted him to concoct what he wanted me to say for the sake of a story, put quotation marks around the words, made me out to be a gullible fool, and persuaded a reputable newspaper to print it as truth. I find the implications of that very disturbing indeed.

Later that same week, the boot really went in again when one of the woman feature-writers in the same paper, assuming, I suppose, the accuracy of the story, referred to me with my 'pink eyes, crying all the way to the bank' because of such a great publicity stunt. 'Honky Tonk Angel' was to sell millions, she reckoned. Happily, the lady was wrong and she's yet to learn what it is that constitutes effective promotion.

The other instance was a piece of diabolical reporting by someone from the *Yorkshire Post*. We were presenting a gospel concert for Tear Fund at the Leeds Town Hall, and usually on occasions like that we try to fit in half an hour or so before the first show to speak to local press and radio. There's no

Every face tells a story! TOP LEFT Gracie Fields was a surprise backstage visitor during a Palladium panto season.

advantage as far as ticket sales are concerned, as we're on our way to the next date before the papers are out. However, the press are usually keen to carry interviews and it's a useful promotional opportunity for Tear Fund. At least, usually!

I think there were about four people at this particular press conference – two local and hospital radio guys with tape-recorders, and two reporters. I did the tape chat first and answered questions about the content of the concert, my involvement with Tear Fund, what Tear Fund was, what project the proceeds would go to, and so on. We covered the ground pretty thoroughly and at the end the reporters didn't want to ask much more.

When the conference had broken up but while the pressmen were still hanging about, one of the concert organisers, I think it was, asked me if I knew that adjacent to the concert hall was the courtroom where the much-publicised Poulson trial had taken place. I didn't know and used one of my overworked superlatives, like 'Amazing'. Below, I was told, was a whole labyrinth of cells which, if there was time, they'd persuade the police to show me.

That was the gist of a two-minute exchange. But for the *Yorkshire Post* reporter, it was news. More important than 3,000 people attending the concerts, more significant than the £3,000 going towards a medical programme in Rwanda, more topical than the purpose that had brought us to Leeds.

I forget the heading but the story ran something like this.' "Did you know, Cliff, that the Poulson case was held here?" Cliff: "Terrific." "Did you know that there are cells under here where prisoners are kept?" Cliff: "Amazing." "Do you know the concert hall is surrounded by courtrooms?' Cliff: "Fantastic." ' And so it went on – nothing about the needs of a developing country, nothing about the Christian gospel, nothing about a Christian organisation that's stabbing out into the world and challenging our apathy – none of that was even hinted. Instead, an ego trip for the writer, a comedy article at my expense, another example of illegitimate, sub-standard journalism.

Can you wonder why, after rubbish like that, I feel sore – even embarrassed to walk out in case people have read it, believed it and thought what a twit I must be. Fortunately the majority of the public are reasonably discerning and take what they read with a pinch of salt. There are some, though, who'll swallow anything and neither I nor anyone else will persuade them that the paper may be wrong!

Usually, in the event of some major press hassle, I try to rush to the nearest TV chat show and put the record straight. On TV I can be myself, say what I want to say in its proper context, and let the audience judge the facts for themselves. When that's not possible, I live through the frustration, telling myself that in a couple of weeks the article will be forgotten and people will be reading some other saga. I just have to hope that the new one is more truthful.

You know where you stand better, of course, with straightforward concert or show criticisms. Early on in show-business you learn to take the rough with the smooth and I've had a fair share of both extremes. Critics are entitled to their opinions, and, as long as it's clear that that's all it is, then fair do's.

Again, I can't pretend that bad reviews don't upset me – they do. All performers want their work to be appreciated and when it's torn to shreds eloquently and publicly the effect can be demoralising. But I would like to see criticism occasionally which takes some account of audience reaction.

A critic at one of my shows, for instance, may be some terrific intellectual who finds 'Congratulations' way below his dignity and hasn't the slightest inclination to smile or clap. But maybe it's just possible that the other 1,999 in the audience may feel differently and actually show their enthusiasm. Isn't it a matter then of being fair and balanced?

If I were criticising someone negatively, I'd want to say, 'OK, I didn't like the song for such-and-such a reason, I don't think he can play guitar, and I don't like his voice, *but* I was obviously in a minority because the audience had a ball.' Instead of that, I've done concerts to packed houses, had fabulous audiences chanting for more when I've left the stage, and yet you'd mistake the write-up next morning for an obituary notice.

In the end, it all boils down to the particular bias of the writer. If he comes with his mind already made up, and he likes neither you, your music, nor what you stand for, then you can bet your life that prejudice will blaze through, no matter how good the performance. Vice versa if he's already sympathetic – then the odds are there'll be a favourable write-up. Believe it or not, I do have a lot of respect for certain critics and reporters whose writing is objective and impartial, but you know how it is – the rotten ones stick!

Theoretically, I suppose, I should get more up-tight about criticism which comes from Christians – I was going to say Christian criticism but I don't mean that! The kind, for instance, that arrived on my doormat this morning. At the top of the page was a verse from the Psalms: 'God is my refuge and strength.' 'Dear Clifford', the letter began, which, unless it's a joke, tells me a fair bit about the writer.

'Since I have heard that you class yourself as also being a born-again member of the body of Jesus Christ, I would like to ask you how you

OVERLEAF Nostalgia was thick in the air for our 20th anniversary reunion at the Palladium in '78.

reconcile the fact that you call yourself a Christian and also sing pop songs. Surely you are an enemy of the cross of Christ if you even consider that you can have any dealings with this filthy world. Please consider what harm you are doing to the Christian youth and non-Christian youth of this land by even suggesting that a follower of Jesus Christ can be so full of compromise.'

I don't get many of those, and for every one there are usually dozens which express love and encouragement. That ensures that I keep a proper perspective. I think I'm enough of a realist too to recognise that within God's family there are plenty of hang-ups, and I'm a sitting target for a good many of them.

Maybe my skin *is* getting tougher, for the most I feel nowadays after reading correspondence like this is disappointment – disappointment that the writer has missed so much of what I've found liberating about the gospel.

In the final analysis, what matters to me is my relationship with the Lord and I know that at this moment I'm as right with Him as I can be. In that respect, what another Christian thinks about me from a distance is relatively unimportant, because it's not going to change my relationship with Jesus one jot. I just say to the Lord how sad it is that a person thinks less of my testimony because of an uninformed opinion. I can get over that in one prayer!

On more of a general principle, it is sad that there are Christians ready to write and speak destructively of other Christians without being absolutely certain that they know the whole balanced truth. We need to be ahead of the non-Christian world in our broadmindedness (not compromise) and in our acceptance of other people. Instead of that, some of us give the impression of being only too keen for a verbal set-to.

I have a sneaky suspicion that I'm probably a shade more vulnerable than most to criticism. The fact is that I like people to agree with me. When they don't, I am disappointed, frustrated and, to my shame, sometimes angry. Even in personal conversation I find myself getting edgy when someone takes a differing view on some issue. I'd be absolutely useless in a formal debate – I could never argue coolly and dispassionately. What I feel and believe, I want other people to feel and believe with me. In talking about Christian things particularly I know that this is a real flaw.

There have been times when I've found it hard to curb feelings of anger when someone has poured scorn on something I believe, or has stubbornly refused to accept a point which, to my mind, is crystal-clear and beyond dispute. With hindsight, I know what a poor witness that is and I see it as a weakness that I have to deal with. Somehow I have to bring together my own dogmatic faith – and truth *is* dogmatic and not wishy-washy – with a tolerance of the other person's point of view.

I reckon I made one step forward during my last trip to Japan. One of my musicians is into a meditative 'all paths lead to God' kind of philosophy and one day I sat and listened to him. That in itself was an achievement, because I'm not a good listener. I prefer to answer the questions rather than ask them and that's another juicy character blemish and another story. Nevertheless, on that occasion I listened and I was impressed with the reasoning and with the thoroughness by which he'd arrived at his position. I still disagreed but I kept my cool. There was no argument and the mutual respect grew by a mile.

I remember in English lessons at school having to write character studies – an old-age pensioner maybe, or the boss of some multi-million business empire. If I'd concocted one on a pop star in those days, I suppose I might have made some reference to his being a show-off or bigheaded.

It's still a popular assumption that everyone who has 'made it' in show-business is inevitably self-opinionated. Now I find it well-nigh impossible to do a kind of psychiatrist's couch act on myself and discover to what extent my behaviour stems from ego and conceit and how much is legitimate enthusiasm and conviction. Personally I believe that I focused show-business and my career in a fairly healthy perspective a long time ago. I live under no delusions in that respect. It could be said that there's a vanity, an egotism, in every performer in that their purpose is to present themselves, but the same could be said of every preacher.

My own minister is a superbly gifted communicator and the Lord uses him and speaks through him, but in the pulpit the man doesn't become a zombie, devoid of personality – quite the opposite. It's the personality, the humour and the attractiveness of the man that are part of his message. In my case, I professionally use my personality to entertain rather than to minister. As I've remarked before, I believe that's just as valid a calling.

Nevertheless, I don't doubt that, after nearly twenty years of being publicly talked about, stared at, given preferential treatment and flattered, something unattractive has rubbed off and left its mark. But for that you'd best ask someone who understands me better than I do! If you do however, just make sure I'm there to put the other side too!

Bill, for instance, would say I'm a bad loser. In one sense, he's right. Everything I do I want to be good at and if I'm lousy I get frustrated and give up. 'Mastermind' is a case in point. That's that little board game which demands what I'm told are logical step-by-step deductions. I know a girl of ten who's brilliant at it, yet I don't begin to fathom how she arrives at her answers. My attempts lead to frustration so I give up. Bill says it's my pride that's hurt; I maintain that it's an awareness of my limitations. Why waste time on chasing things you can't do when there's more satisfaction to be gained from things you can? Mind you, I still occasionally have a go at 'Mastermind'!

Funnily enough, I didn't mind losing the Eurovision Song Contests. Well, that's not quite true. Admittedly, the first time was a disappointment, particularly as everyone was convinced we would walk away with it, and particularly as the winner was such a duff song.

Even Katie Boyle demanded a re-count because she couldn't believe the result herself, and she was supposed to be the unbiased commère.

But with 'Power to all our friends' I knew we had a great song and that, whether we won or lost, it would be a smash hit. I remember telling my band that the only way to treat the Contest was as the biggest plug anyone could give their latest record. Four hundred million people were watching – a sort of world 'Top of the Pops'. Sure enough, we lost, but sold one and a half million copies.

It puzzles me now when people suggest that Eurovision may have harmed my career. Personally I can't see it. If the records had flopped, maybe; but both 'Congratulations', which has become a celebration standard, and 'Power' resulted in gold discs and a vast amount of airplay throughout Europe. If that's harm, who needs success?

Even so, I can't pretend that those contests weren't nerve-racking. The most torturous part is waiting with the other performers as results are announced and the TV cameras shoot close-ups of the strain. I couldn't face that, and went to the loo for the crucial quarter of an hour. My manager called me when it was over, and broke the news.

It seems to surprise people to hear that I still get butterflies before a public appearance. I wish I didn't. The theory about nerves improving a performance is nonsense, in my case at least. All they do is cause tension in the throat and a below-par performance. There's not a scrap of doubt that my singing is better in the relaxed easy atmosphere of a recording studio than in front of TV cameras and an audience of a few million.

In the early days, I used to make myself literally sick with nerves. I'd develop a really deep fruity cough which would tear my throat and my insides apart, but would disappear the minute I got on stage. Nowadays the cough isn't so troublesome, but I freeze instead. I think I'm a cold mortal at the best of times, but when others are loosening their ties and jackets in steamy dressing rooms, I'm trying to keep the circulation going and stop the teeth from chattering.

Some of my worst nerves are before a Christian meeting. Maybe it's because there's more at stake – I don't know – but, humanly speaking, I'd prefer to face 3,000 people at the Palladium for two hours, rather than 500 for half an hour at a church or a university. The extra heating bills that churches have had to fork out because I've needed the electric fire going full blast in the vicar's vestry must add up to a tidy sum.

Then, if there's some really big occasion looming up, like a tour involving a new act, or a new TV series, I develop a sleep problem. At least I've discovered a solution that's better than tablets – Goon records.

This is what you do: get yourself a portable record-player, position it within easy arm's reach of the bed and, as soon as your mind starts latching on to future problems, start playing a comedy LP – my preference is the Goons or Tony Hancock – it really doesn't matter as long as it talks. I can't promise what effect it will have on you; all I know is that before the end of the album I'll come over all drowsy and, hey presto, it's morning. It's a great technique, so long as you can afford new batteries twice a week. The point is you have to listen to the chat and that takes your mind off absolutely everything else. I met Hatti Jacques once and put my foot in it by telling her that she and Hancock sent me to sleep!

Then there was the recurring nightmare – I say 'was' because hopefully it belongs to the past. It usually involved the Shadows. We'd be on stage somewhere and every note they played was deliberately ghastly; for them the show would start as a huge joke, which gradually deteriorated into total shambles. I'd be out there in front trying to pacify the audience but one by one they left, till the theatre was deserted. I'd wake up in a cold sweat, abandoned, in a deserted bedroom!

Similarly, during my occasional ventures into acting, I've had what must be the classic nightmare for all actors – arriving at opening night without learning the lines. For some reason, I'd missed all the rehearsals but was expected to take part in the actual performances just the same. When it came to curtain-up, I didn't know what part I was to play or even what the plot was. The best I could do was ad lib and hope for the best. That, let me promise you, is a five-star nightmare!

Partly at least it must be the nervous tension which causes many showbiz people to be very heavy smokers. Not so with me. It's nothing to do with will-power and self-discipline but fortunately, even as a kid, I detested the smell of cigarette smoke and ash, and never even got as far as a sly schoolboy drag.

I remember as a child being asked by my father, who smoked quite heavily, to pass an ashtray and I used to nudge Donna, because I couldn't stand the sight or smell of it. The thought of having the smell on my fingers was unbearable and there was no way anyone could persuade me to taste it. Today I detest it no less and, even if some one-in-a-million acting chance cropped up which required me to smoke, I'd have to turn it down.

Of course I've come to terms with it in others. I'm surrounded every day by people who smoke heavily and I wouldn't dream of asking them to put out their cigarette, although I can't pretend I don't mind. I know for a fact that my voice has gone on three or four occasions after prolonged times in smoky atmospheres, and the very thought of inhaling smoke that others have puffed out is foul.

In case you haven't guessed, I look on smoking as unhealthy, unnatural and anti-social – I wish the world would abandon it!

Thankfully it's only been a bit of throat trouble, an occupational hazard, and, more recently, a dodgy back which have given rise to any health worries. Needless to say, having to pull out of a commitment at the last minute is a traumatic business, not just for me but for everyone involved in organisation and promotion. Fortunately it's happened very rarely and insurance-wise I'm regarded as a low-category risk.

What I dread is that wayward fifth lumbar causing trouble in the middle of a tour. I did six TV shows a while back with a disc out, wearing one of those steel corsets to hold me upright, but it was agony and there's no way I could have done a two-hour stage act, even if I'd stood motionless at the microphone.

However, so far it's popped out at relatively convenient points in the schedule and hopefully, with the discovery of a good chiropractor and with plenty of swimming exercise in the pool at home, we'll have it beaten. Less frequently lumbared, you might say!

15 Converging Paths

I WISH I HAD a neat well-rounded conclusion for you. I remember my English teacher drumming into me that every sound piece of writing needed a beginning, a middle and an end. So much for the theory. Maybe the book should have waited another twenty years. Maybe there'll be a sequel – *Which One's Cliff? Part II*. The point is that, instead of a tailor-made tucking-up of ends, I've an inkling that spiritually and professionally I'm still on the threshold.

Career-wise, 1976 was a watershed. One music paper described it as 'the year of the Cliff Richard renaissance'. It wasn't just that I had renewed recording success, or even that at long last I cracked the American bogey with 'Devil Woman'. What was significant, possibly more significant than anything I've done since I stopped trying to imitate Elvis, was that people in the business sat up and started taking my music seriously.

The bombshell arrived with 'I'm Nearly Famous', an album which within months launched at least three hit singles in dozens of countries around the world and became my first entry in the UK album charts for years. I don't know about Bruce Welch, who produced the album and ferreted around for the numbers, but when I went into the studio I didn't consciously plan to try anything different. I certainly loved the songs that we eventually whittled down from Bruce's short-list and I appreciated the kind of freshness about the style and mood of the new material. The funny thing was that 'Devil Woman' had been around my music room for eighteen months or more before Bruce heard it and spotted the potential.

It wasn't until we were halfway through recording sessions that I realised something new was happening. I was interpreting songs like 'Miss You Nights', 'Devil Woman', and 'Can't Ask for Anything More than You' in a way that for me was more ambitious and uninhibited. In that last number, for instance, I sang half the thing falsetto – something I'd never dared, or maybe never had the opportunity, to do on disc before.

Six months later, when I did the song on 'Top of the Pops', one kid, when he saw it was me, turned to his Dad and said, 'Cor, is it 'im singing? I thought it was some black bloke!'

OVERLEAF, ABOVE When performing with dancers, the trick is to make the same shapes as they do.

BELOW Filming 'His Land' in Israel was the best location ever.

I shared the platform with Billy Graham during 'Spree' – a memorable series of meetings at Earl's Court.

Who loves, ya, baby?

Not the kind of line-up I'm used to, but the Boys' Brigade put on an impressive display at the Wembley Pool. As a Brigade Vice-President, I was guest of honour.

No caption necessary!

The reaction more or less world wide to 'I'm Nearly Famous' was fantastic. EMI went overboard and, for the first time I can remember, pulled out all the promotion stops. 'I'm Nearly Famous' tee-shirts started appearing in all the 'in' places; DJs began shaving in 'I'm Nearly Famous' mirrors; and no less a duo than Elizabeth Taylor and Elton John were pictured sporting 'I'm Nearly Famous' buttons at a Philadelphia reception.

Actually it was Elton's own enthusiasm, together with the efforts of Rocket Records, that put 'Miss You Nights' and 'Devil Woman' on the road in the States in the first place. I gather that Elton was so determined to get the discs heard that he hawked them around personally and showed as much concern about them as for his own current releases. Elton's mother once told me that her son had been a Cliff fan ever since she took him to a Palladium pantomime when he was thirteen. With fans like that, who needs agents!

I felt tremendously excited at having cracked America. I can't pretend I wasn't. The fact that I did it on my terms, without a long stint in Las Vegas, and without trudging around month after month, promoting and performing and meeting the right people, gave an added perverse satisfaction. As I say, I'm grateful to Rocket Records, whose label I now record for in America. Their absolute conviction that we'd succeed, together with initiative, hard work and enthusiasm, was remarkable and something I'd never encountered before in quite that intensity. Getting those weekly calls from Los Angeles as 'Devil Woman' progressed, with a weekly 'bullet' up the charts, was like starting my career all over again. The fact that the record company genuinely shared in the excitement and the satisfaction, for my sake as well as for theirs, was a bonus.

One interesting assumption on the part of many people, both in and out of the business, was that Stateside success inevitably meant that I'd be following hot on the heels of Engelbert, Tom Jones, and Olivia Newton-John and find a home in America. Even when I put them right and told them I hadn't the slightest inclination to live in the States – or anywhere else outside England, come to that – there was a kind of 'wink, wink, nudge, nudge' reaction as though to say 'Who are you kidding?'

They can believe what they like, of course, but the truth is that America doesn't entice one bit. Although I've enjoyed previous visits, have some good and valued American friends, and recognise all the professional and financial advantages, I could never settle or be happy there. I don't know enough about the place to make harsh judgments but my superficial impression is negative. If you live and breathe showbiz and music, OK, it makes sense; but home will always be England and I certainly don't intend letting the tax-man chase me away!

What recent successes have done is to clarify in my own mind what kind of showbiz animal I am and basically, let's face it, I'm a pop singer with roots unashamedly in rock 'n roll. That hasn't ruled out other things in the past and it won't in the future, but I'm beginning to realise more and more that, if you set your sights on one specific area of entertainment, the probability is that other areas will disregard you. Even a year ago I thought I could have a go at everything. Why shouldn't I act now and then? Sing now and then? Do television occasionally? And venture every so often into comedy? Why not try my hand as a record producer? Now I'm not so sure. Certainly if a film part came up that offered a genuine acting role and wasn't another red bus substitute, I'd do it, but I'm aware too that the longer I leave the gaps between straight acting the harder it will be to land a worthwhile part.

It's the same with record producing. I've learned that a good producer is a full-time producer; you've got to be able and willing to spend a lot of time looking for appropriate songs – anything less does your artist an injustice. At present I can't give it that priority.

Maybe, you see, in my heart of hearts, I am a rock 'n roll man and want to get back to what I originally set out to be. Even if I clip my wings, concentrate more on rock 'n roll, and cut down on the rest, the 'general entertainer' image in Britain is reasonably safe. The Palladium pantomimes and variety shows, the cabaret and the TV series – they've all been an integral part of my career and there's no thought of renouncing any of it. The problem is that those areas in themselves limit me to an audience that demands 'The Young Ones' and 'Congratulations', and that can be professionally stifling.

In the very first instance, my audience joined me on a rock 'n roll ticket and, if live concerts today are anything to judge by, it's still the rock 'n roll numbers that grab them more than anything. In a way, the circle's come full turn. In the early days, after 'Move it', it was more commercial to do cover jobs such as 'Twelfth of Never' and 'It's All in the Game' – beautiful songs but at the opposite end of the pop spectrum. Then the rock 'n roll stuff dried up, people tagged me as a ballad singer, and that's more or less how it was till Bruce unearthed the material for 'I'm Nearly Famous'. Ironically, since my return to the music I initially loved best of all, I've had more sales and reaction than anything I've recorded in the last ten years.

Today I feel as though I've rediscovered ninety per cent of my career. I've always enjoyed recording but there was a lull for a long time. I'd arrive punctually at the studio; Norrie or Dave Mackay would have seen to the backing track; I'd sing the song, and that was it. Maybe one song would take an hour, at the most two. The difference now is that I'm involved. 'I'm Nearly Famous' involved me in the selection of songs, in the arrangements, in the vocal group, and in the mixing, and it was like it used to be fifteen years ago. If I needed rejuvenating, it did the trick. At the moment I can't wait to get back in the studio – if only to prove it was no flash in the pan.

And the easiest thing in the world for me would be to relax into it and be totally engulfed. There's a verse in the New Testament that says 'If any man thinks that he stands, let him take heed lest he fall!' I'm aware of the dangers; I'm aware that Satan can use success and fame and music and things which in themselves are neither good nor bad to undermine and destroy. Sometimes I cast an envious eye at someone like Brother Andrew, a man solely dependent on his faith, and find myself wondering how my faith would cope if I didn't have my career. I'd like to think it would stand but at present I know full well that for many practical things it's my career I depend on, not the Lord.

Certainly faith makes the rest of life worthwhile but then I have got the rest of life going for me. I *do* have success at human material level. God seems to have permitted it and I don't despise it – quite the contrary – but, boy, it needs a lot of prayer and a lot of grace to keep it in proper perspective. If ever the time came when I found myself serving my career, instead of my career serving me, then I'd know it was time to get out. I only hope I'd have the discernment to realise it.

Meanwhile, as the career goes into a new phase, I believe there are new doors to go through spiritually. I'm aware more than anyone that God has to do a great deal more with me yet before I can do the job He intends. Eleven years as a Christian have shaped and turned me from a fairly selfish, unthinking person to a slightly less selfish – we're never going to get out of the pride business completely in this life – and considerably more thoughtful one.

But I can love a lot more than I love, I can know a lot more than I know and I can walk a lot more closely to Christ than I do. For that I need His help and His grace, and I need the support and the prayers of other Christians. A few months ago a Christian youth leader asked me whether I found being the leading Christian ambassador to the present generation a formidable responsibility. They were his words, not mine and they sent me into a kind of nervous chill. I think I said that if I really believed I had that role, I'd disappear underground.

The scary thing is that, on reflection, I realise some people may actually see me in that light. In one sense I believe they're mistaken, because I could name dozens of men and women who I know full well are better ambassadors, better reflections of their Master, than I am. To my mind though, there's a danger in trying to pin a label like that on anyone.

In the eyes of the world, understandably, there is a handful of Christian people who are seen and heard communicating more than others. I have probably spoken more on television about Christian things than anyone else, and I've probably had more interviews with the press than most. But all my ammunition comes from those who teach me.

It's the same as when Paul said, 'Are you baptised of Paul or Peter? You're not. We're all baptised of the Lord and we've all got our different and equally important roles to play. We are all organs of the same body.' So the danger in looking to someone as a leader is that that person takes on an unreal importance. I know that I have the privilege of a terrific career from which there's a superb platform. I can actually witness to the reality of Jesus through television, records, films and radio, but I merely give out what has already been said, and said much better, by other people who don't have the same media opportunities.

Yet, when all's said and done, I have to accept that my responsibility, humanly speaking, is different from Joe Bloggs who can nestle anonymously week by week in some suburban evangelical pew. Make no mistake, Joe Bloggs is an ambassador for Christ in his situation no less than I am in mine. But if Joe Bloggs makes a mistake, the repercussions go no further than those who know him. If I make a mistake, the whole world is likely to hear pretty smartly, and you can bet your life that the world's first retort will be, 'And he calls himself a Christian!' If I do slip up and say the wrong thing, if I do get involved in anything that would be considered un-Christian, it would be Christ who would suffer, Christ who would be judged, and I find that painful. Yet I've no option – I can't opt out.

Peter and John told the Jewish council, 'We cannot stop telling about the wonderful things which we saw Jesus do and heard Him say.' I know just what they meant and there's no way that I can clam up either, and when I speak I'm reported – that's the situation and if I don't like it I'd better quit show-business, retreat from public life altogether, and join Joe Bloggs in the pew. I'd find another ministry, no doubt, but what a surrender and what a motive for ducking out!

I'm left, of course, absolutely dependent on God to keep His side of the bargain. If He isn't able to give me the words and the common-sense at the moment when mine run out then I've no chance. If He isn't able to 'keep me from falling', as the Bible says He is, even when my feet are slithering and dithering all over the place, then again the press might as well start writing their headlines now. The fact is I've discovered that God is faithful and His promises are actually reliable. Time and time again I've proved it.

Imagine how I felt when Billy Graham invited me to a supper party, along with two or three eminent politicians, Sir Alec Douglas-Home among them, and two members of the Royal Family. Think of it – just Billy, the Royal couple, a batch of statesmen, and Cliff Richard! Talk about feeling inadequate!

I knew that if politics were on the agenda I'd be a non-starter, but Billy said he'd like me there, the diary was clear, and that kind of opportunity doesn't crop up every week. So I went and discovered a freedom and a confidence that I'd never imagined possible in that company. Within minutes of the meal ending, the discussion veered towards God, and that's where it stayed, and there was I with as much to contribute as anyone! For certain, Billy was responsible for the relaxed and friendly atmosphere, but Billy didn't give me the words to speak. Theoretically I believe they came from God; from experience I know they did!

The lesson I learned that evening, by the way, is that the Christian knows more about his belief than the non-Christian does about his unbelief. I was staggered at the time but have found the same thing over and over again: no matter how brilliant or important or experienced are the people you're talking to, if they don't know Christ, they're at a disadvantage. You have something positive to offer; they have nothing.

Billy's supper party was a unique occasion but I've gone into literally scores of situations – meetings, interviews or whatever – feeling spiritually apathetic, Jesus has seemed distant, and the Bible dreary. All I've been able to do is to remind God that I'm His representative and that it's up to Him to see me through. Without exception, the moment I've opened my mouth, the moment I've got into the reason for it all, that mood has gone and the words come, and I'm convinced that that's God the Holy Spirit doing what He said He would, keeping His side of the bargain.

But what about my side? I see that very simply as a need to keep in touch and do what some wise old Christian hundreds of years ago described as 'practising the presence of God'. That sounds a bit pompous and high-falutin' but all he meant, I think, was a willingness to bring God into your day, in all sorts of mundane and ordinary situations.

I'm a great believer in SOS prayers, those odd things we share with God that suddenly come to mind when we're driving the car, for instance, or in my case preparing backstage in a dressing room. There's no need to close your eyes, kneel down, face east or anything else – what's important is that God is so much part and parcel of life that spontaneous mental chat becomes second nature.

Personally I find that easier than setting aside a formal time each day for some Bible study and rather more serious prayer. That needs discipline, and organising my time is something I happily leave to others. But I'm convinced there'll be no semblance of Christian growth without it and at home I've no excuse. On tour it's more tricky – the whole hassle of late concerts, midnight meals, and long conversations means I crawl into bed pretty shattered and any attempt at concentration is futile. What I have to do then is shuffle the routine round a bit and fit in a time in the morning or as soon as we arrive at a new hotel in the afternoon.

Even when I'm wide awake I don't find prayer an easy thing. Like everyone else, I imagine, my mind tends to gallop all over the place and sometimes there's that awful sensation of non-communication, as though I'm speaking to a brick wall. Probably more often than not, the fault lies squarely with me but it's dawned on me recently that Satan must do his level best to sabotage every effort we make to get through to God. Our line must be well and truly bugged and I imagine all the stops are out to achieve a blockage.

In itself, the very awareness that Satan is listening in has helped. I can now denounce him right from the start and I've taken to sometimes actually mouthing and speaking my prayers instead of just thinking them. That's vastly helped my concentration, although goodness knows what it's done for anyone eavesdropping through the hotel walls!

I find that a prayer list helps again to keep my mind on the job. There are dozens of people for whom I feel responsible, for one reason or another, to pray for regularly; there are matters concerning Tear Fund and the Arts Centre; certain things that other people have asked me to pray about; and a whole string of subjects quite apart from family and personal situations. The only way I can hope to cover everything is to have some sort of reminder system; a list tucked in my Bible does the trick. I don't begin to get through it each day but over the course of a week or so I can be sure nothing gets forgotten.

There are some who take exception to being 'used'. The very term evokes an idea of taking advantage or cashing in at someone's expense. Being used by God isn't like that; if I'm used, the advantage in terms of fulfilment and happiness is mine; the expense is always God's. My ambition is to be used more; used in whatever way, in whatever place, He makes possible.

OK, so as far as the Church and its PR are concerned, Cliff Richard is a commodity – that doesn't bother me. What I want to ask, as part of the Church, is what is the very best way, the most God-honouring way, to use that commodity? To date it's been in pre-evangelism, an ugly label but I can't think of a better one. Although I gather there have been times when God has brought about conversions as a result of something I've said, I don't see my role primarily as an evangelist.

For a start, I would question how responsible it would be for me, a pop

singer, to encourage on-the-spot commitments to Christ from a public
platform, when I know there are many emotional and psychological factors
at work which are distracting and deceiving. Far better, I feel, to leave
public evangelism to those who feel clearly led to it and who communicate
to people's minds, emotions and souls on the one spiritual level.

What I mean by pre-evangelism is chat that sparks people into genuine
honest thinking. That can take many forms – sometimes it's just a word or
two or testimony in a concert or during a Talk of the Town performance;
sometimes it's through reasons for my faith, and facts about Jesus and sin
and salvation, spelt out in gospel concerts or in dialogue sessions in church
or college; sometimes it's via the occasional over-dinner or party
conversation, when curious and maybe slightly envious guests start
pummelling me with questions. There's rarely a neat conclusion; seldom,
if ever, has anyone said, 'I want to become a Christian now; show me what
to do.' More often than not, when I leave the theatre or church or the
restaurant, I hear no more and I wonder whether anything was achieved.
Just occasionally, however, I get the thrill of hearing about someone who
began their seeking as a result of something I said, and maybe months or
even years later, another Christian has had the privilege of leading him or
her into our Family.

The fact that I don't have much of a personal counselling ministry is
something else that apparently upsets other Christians more than it does
me. It's back to the Bible's 'body' illustration again and all I can assume is
that we've a long way to go before really grasping the principle of differing
roles. We're not intended to be carbon copies of one another, and thank
goodness we're not. Never in a month of Sundays, for instance, could I do
what Arthur Blessitt does. The thought of leaving a dressing room covered
in 'Jesus loves you' stickers appals me and I could no more go up to a TV
camera-man and hand him a tract than fly, but Arthur Blessitt would, and
he'd get away with it because for him it's right and if he didn't witness in
that extrovert way he'd be untrue to himself, as well as to God who gave
him his personality.

But even in less extreme situations I'm still doubtful about the wisdom
of a 'personal ministry', as Christians would call it. It's all too easy to be
taken for a ride by the sweet young lady who comes to the house and wants
me to help her find God. Maybe I'm wrong, but my advice to her is to
contact her local minister! There's no armchair treatment or a cup of tea!

Some may interpret that as unfriendly and aloof; through my eyes there's
a different perspective. Inevitably anyone who earns his living on the stage
has to be an impersonal kind of person: he appears on stage, the spotlight
hits him, and 2,000 people sit in their dark corners and watch and listen

from a distance. Now if I'm not Cliff Richard by accident, if my career was planned or predestined, as I believe it was, then I must accept the impersonal relationship. Most people – the public, if you like – I meet only at arm's length; hopefully there's as valid a ministry at arm's length as there is over a teacup!

Now, just one practical suggestion. I have no doubt that there are masses of people around with nagging questions in their minds about religion, and about Christianity in particular, but who haven't a clue where to turn easily and without embarrassment for answers. In case you're in that predicament and can't summon enough enthusiasm to collar your local clergyman, then drop a line – with a stamped addressed envelope – to Millmead Centre, Guildford, Surrey, and my friends there will do their best to put you in touch with someone who can help. Please understand that they are not able to deal with any queries relating to me – but if you honestly want to understand more about Jesus then do make contact.

What of the future then? Selfishly, I'd love to think that audiences will become more tolerant and allow me to be wholly me on stage. In other words, that Christians and non-Christians alike would be sufficiently broad-minded to allow me to express my music and my faith without forcing me to departmentalise Christian and secular. What a relief it would be to go on stage without having to worry whether I would offend either the godly or the pagans by what I was singing or saying! But I guess that's a pipe-dream.

What I really want is to be seen to actually be this Christian that I claim I am. Not so that people will say, 'What a sincere bloke Cliff Richard is', but simply so that Jesus will get noticed. What other people think of me is becoming less and less important; what they think of Jesus because of me is critical.

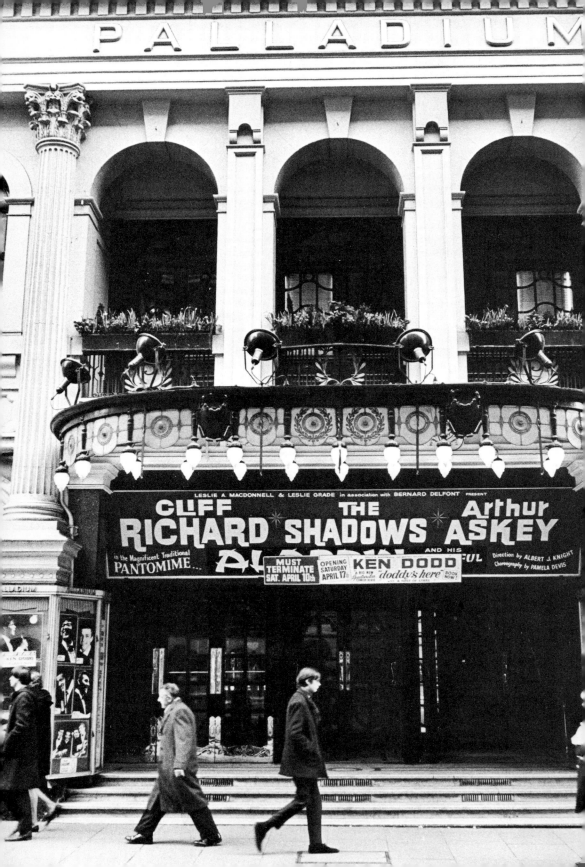

Cliff Richard Discography

Singles	*Released*
Move It/Schoolboy Crush	August 1958
High Class Baby/My Feet Hit The Ground	November 1958
Livin' Lovin' Doll/Steady With You	January 1959
Mean Streak/Never Mind	April 1959
Living Doll/Apron Strings	July 1959
Travellin' Light/Dynamite	October 1959
A Voice in the Wilderness/Don't Be Mad At Me	January 1960
Fall In Love With You/Willie And The Hand Jive	March 1960
Please Don't Tease/Where Is My Heart	June 1960
Nine Times Out of Ten/Thinking Of Our Love	September 1960
I Love You/'D' In Love	December 1960
Theme For A Dream/Mumblin' Mosie	February 1961
A Girl Like You/Now's The Time To Fall In Love	June 1961
Gee Whiz It's You/I Cannot Find A True Love	August 1961
When The Girl In Your Arms Is The Girl In Your Heart/ Got A Funny Feeling	October 1961
The Young Ones/We Say Yeah	January 1962
I'm Lookin' Out The Window/Do You Want to Dance	May 1962
It'll Be Me/Since I Lost You	August 1962
The Next Time/Bachelor Boy	November 1962
Summer Holiday/Dancing Shoes	February 1963
Lucky Lips/I Wonder	May 1963
It's All In The Game/ Your Eyes Tell On You	August 1963
Don't Talk To Him/Say You're Mine	November 1963
I'm The Lonely One/Watch What You Do With My Baby	January 1964
Constantly/True Lovin'	April 1964
On The Beach/A Matter of Moments	June 1964
The Twelfth Of Never/I'm Afraid To Go Home	October 1964
I Could Easily Fall In Love With You/ I'm In Love With You	November 1964
The Minute You're Gone/Just Another Guy	March 1965
On My Word/Just A Little Bit Too Late	June 1965
Time In Between/Look Before You Love	August 1965
Wind Me Up (Let Me Go)/The Night	October 1965
Blue Turns To Grey/Somebody Loses	February 1966
Visions/What Would I Do (For The Love Of A Girl)	July 1966
Time Drags By/La La La Song	October 1966

The governor of all theatres – the London Palladium – for pantos and 20th anniversary nostalgia!

In The Country/Finders Keepers	December 1966
It's All Over/Why Wasn't I Born Rich	March 1967
I'll Come Runnin'/I Get The Feelin'	June 1967
The Day I Met Marie/Our Story Book	September 1967
All My Love/Sweet Little Jesus Boy	November 1967
Congratulations/High 'n Dry	March 1968
I'll Love You Forever Today/ Girl You'll Be A Woman Soon	June 1968
Marianne/Mr. Nice	September 1968
Don't Forget To Catch Me/What's More (I Don't Need Her)	November 1968
Good Times/Occasional Rain	February 1969
Big Ship/She's Leaving You	May 1969
Throw Down A Line/Reflections (Cliff & Hank)	September 1969
With The Eyes Of A Child/So Long	November 1969
The Joy Of Living/Boogatoo, Leave My Woman Alone	February 1970
Goodbye Sam Hello Samantha/ You Never Can Tell	May 1970
I Ain't Got Time Anymore/Monday Comes Too Soon	August 1970
Sunny Honey Girl/Don't Move Away (Cliff & Olivia) /I Was Only Fooling Myself	January 1971
Silvery Rain/Annabella Umberella/Time Flies	March 1971
Flying Machine/Pigeon	June 1971
Sing A Song Of Freedom/A Thousand Conversations	October 1971
Jesus/Mr. Cloud	February 1972
Living In Harmony/Empty Chairs	August 1972
Brand New Song/The Old Accordion	November 1972
Power To All Our Friends/Come Back Billie Joe	March 1973
Help It Along/Tomorrow Rising/The Days Of Love/ Ashes To Ashes	April 1973
Take Me High/Celestial Houses	November 1973
(You Keep Me) Hanging On/Love Is Here	April 1974
It's Only Me You've Left Behind/ You're The One	March 1975
Honky Tonk Angel/Wouldn't You Know It (Got Myself A Girl)	September 1975
Miss You Nights/Love Enough	November 1975
Devil Woman/Love On (Shine On)	April 1976
I Can't Ask For Anymore Than You/Junior Cowboy	July 1976
Hey Mr. Dream Maker/No One Waits	November 1976
My Kinda Life/Nothing Left For Me To Say	February 1977
When Two Worlds Drift Apart/That's Why I Love You	June 1977
Yes He Lives/Good On The Sally Army	January 1978

E.P.'S

Serious Charge   *May 1959*
Living Doll, No Turning Back, Mad About You. (The Shadows: Chinchilla).

Cliff No. 1   *June 1959*
Apron Strings, My Babe, Down The Line, I Gotta Feeling, Baby I Don't Care.

Cliff No. 2   *July 1959*
Donna, Move It, Ready Teddy, Too Much, Don't Bug Me Baby.

Expresso Bongo   *January 1959*
Love, A Voice In The Wilderness, The Shrine On The Second Floor, (The Shadows: Bongo Blues).

Cliff Sings No. 1   *February 1960*
Here Comes Summer, I Gotta Know, Blue Suede Shoes, The Snake And The Bookworm.

Cliff Sings No. 2   *March 1960*
Twenty Flight Rock, Pointed Toe Shoes, Mean Woman Blues, I'm Walkin'.

Cliff Sings No. 3   *June 1960*
I'll String Along With You, Embraceable You, As Times Goes By, The Touch Of Your Lips.

Cliff Sings No. 4   *September 1960*
I Don't Know Why (I Just Do), Little Things Mean A Lot, Somewhere Along The Way, That's My Desire.

Cliff's Silver Discs   *December 1960*
Please Don't Tease, Fall In Love With You, Nine Times Out Of Ten, Travellin' Light.

Me and My Shadows No. 1   *February 1961*
I'm Gonna Get You, You And I, I Cannot Find A True Love, Evergreen Tree, She's Gone.

Me And My Shadows No. 2   *March 1961*
Left Out Again, You're Just The One To Do It, Lamp Of Love, Choppin' 'n Changin', We Have It Made.

Me And My Shadows No. 3   *April 1961*
Tell Me, Gee Whiz It's You, I'm Willing To Learn, I Love You So, I Don't Know.

Listen To Cliff   *October 1961*
What'd I Say, True Love Will Come To You, Blue Moon, Lover.

Dream   *November 1961*
Dream, All I Do Is Dream Of You, I'll See You In My Dreams, Then Grow Too Old To Dream.

Listen To Cliff No. 2   *December 1961*
Unchained Melody, First Lesson In Love, Idle Gossip, Almost Like Being In Love, Beat Out Dat Rhythm On A Drum.

Cliff's Hit Parade   *February 1962*
I Love You, Theme For A Dream, A Girl Like You, When The Girl In Your Arms
Is The Girl In Your Heart.

Cliff Richard No. 1   *April 1962*
Forty Days, Catch Me, How Wonderful To Know, Tough Enough.

Hits From 'The Young Ones'   *May 1962*
The Young Ones, Got A Funny Feeling, Lesson In Love, We Say Yeah.

Cliff Richard No. 2   *June 1962*
50 Tears For Every Kiss, The Night Is So Lonely, Poor Boy, Y'Arriva.

Cliff's Hits   *November 1962*
It'll Be Me, Since I Lost You, Do You Want To Dance, I'm Looking Out The
Window.

Time For Cliff And The Shadows   *March 1963*
So I've Been Told, I'm Walkin' The Blues, When My Dreamboat Comes Home,
Blueberry Hill, You Don't Know.

Holiday Carnival   *May 1963*
Carnival, Moonlight Bay, Some Of These days, For You And Me.

Hits From 'Summer Holiday'   *June 1963*
Summer Holiday, The Next Time, Dancing Shoes, Bachelor Boy.

More Hits From 'Summer Holiday'   *September 1963*
Seven Days To A Holiday, Stranger In Town, Really Waltzing, All At Once.

Cliff's Lucky Lips   *October 1963*
It's All In The Game, Your Eyes Tell On You, Lucky Lips, I Wonder.

Love Songs   *November 1963*
I'm In The Mood For Love, Secret Love, Love Letters, I Only Have Eyes For You.

When In France   *February 1964*
La Mer Boum, J'Attendrai, C'Est Si Bon.

Cliff Sings Don't Talk To Him   *March 1964*
Don't Talk To Him, Say You're Mine, Spanish Harlem, Who Are We To Say,
Falling In Love With Love.

Cliff's Palladium Successes   *May 1964*
I'm The Lonely One, Watch What You Do With My Baby, Perhaps, Perhaps,
Perhaps, Frenesi.

Wonderful Life   *August 1964*
Wonderful Life, Do You Remember, What've I Gotta Do, Walkin'.

A Forever Kind Of Love   September 1964
A Forever Kind Of Love, It's Wonderful To Be Young, Constantly, True, True
Lovin'.

Wonderful Life No. 2   October 1964
Matter Of Moments, Girl In Every Port, A Little Imagination, In The Stars.

Hits From Wonderful Life   December 1964
On The Beach, We Love A Movie, Home, All Kinds Of People.

Why Don't They Understand   February 1965
Why Don't They Understand, Where The Four Winds Blow, The Twelfth Of Never,
I'm Afraid To Go Home.

Cliff's Hits From Aladdin & His Wonderful Lamp   March 1965
Havin' Fun, Evening Comes, Friends, I Could Easily Fall (In Love With You).

Look In My Eyes Maria   May 1965
Look In My Eyes Maria, Where Is Your Heart, Maria, If I Give My Heart To You.

Angel   September 1965
Angel, I Only Came To Say Goodbye, On My Word, The Minute You're Gone.

Take Four   October 1965
Boom Boom, My Heart Is An Open Book, Lies & Kisses, Sweet And Gentle.

Wind Me Up   February 1966
Wind Me Up, The Night, The Time In Between, Look Before You Love.

Hits From When In Rome   April 1966
Come Prima (For The First Time), Nel Blu Dipinto di Blu (Volare), Dicitoncello
Vuve (Just Say I Love Her), Arriverderci Roma.

Love Is Forever   April 1966
My Colouring Book, Fly Me To The Moon, Someday, Everyone Needs Someone
To Love.

La La La La La   December 1966
La La La La La, Solitary Man, Things We Said Today, Never Knew What Love
Could Do.

Cinderella   May 1967
Come Sunday, Peace And Quiet, She Needs Him More Than Me, Hey Doctor Man.

Carol Singers   November 1967
God Rest You Merry Gentlemen, In The Bleak Midwinter, Unto Us A Boy Is Born,
While Shepherds Watched, Little Town of Bethlehem.

L.P.'S   *Released*

Cliff   *April 1959*
Apron Strings, My Babe, Down The Line, I Got A Feeling, Jet Black, (The
Drifters), Baby I Don't Care, Donna, Move It, Ready, Teddy, Too Much, Don't Bug
Me Baby, Driftin' (The Drifters), That'll Be The Day, Be-Bop-A-Lula (The
Drifters), Danny, Whole Lotta Shakin' Goin' On.

Cliff Sings   *November 1959*
Blue Suede Shoes, The Snake And The Bookworm, I Gotta Know, Here Comes
Summer, I'll String Along With You, Embraceable You, As Time Goes By, The
Touch Of Your Lips, Twenty Flight Rock, Pointed Toe Shoes, Mean Woman Blues,
I'm Walking, I Don't Know Why, Little Things Mean A Lot, Somewhere Along
The Way, That's My Desire.

Me And My Shadows   *October 1960*
I'm Gonna Get You, You And I, I Cannot Find A True Love, Evergreen Tree, She's
Gone, Left Out Again, You're Just The One To Do It, Lamp Of Love, Choppin' 'n
Changin', We Have It Made, Tell Me, Gee Whiz It's You, I Love You So, I'm
Willing To Learn, I Don't Know, Working After School.

Listen To Cliff   *May 1961*
What'd I Say, Blue Moon, True Love Will Come To You, Lover, Unchained
Melody, Idle Gossip, First Lesson In Love, Almost Like Being In Love, Beat Out
Dat Rhythm On A Drum, Memories Linger On, Temptation, I Live For You,
Sentimental Journey, I Want You To Know, We Kiss In A Shadow, It's You.

21 Today   *October 1961*
Happy Birthday To You, Forty Days, Catch Me, How Wonderful To Know, Tough
Enough, 50 Tears For Every Kiss, The Night Is So Lonely, Poor Boy, Yarriva,
Outsider, Tea For Two, To Prove My Love For You, Without You, A Mighty
Lonely Man, My Blue Heaven, Shame On You.

The Young Ones   *January 1962*
Friday Night, Got A Funny Feeling, Peace Pipe, Nothing's Impossible, The Young
Ones, All For One, Lessons In Love, No One For Me But Nicky, What D' You
Know We've Got A Show & Vaudeville Routine, When The Girl In Your Arms Is
The Girl In Your Heart, Just Dance, Mood Mambo, The Savage, We Say Yeah.

32 Minutes And 17 Seconds With Cliff Richard   *October 1962*
It'll Be Me, So I've Been Told, How Long Is Forever, I'm Walkin' The Blues, Turn
Around, Blueberry Hill, Let's Make A Memory, When My Dreamboat Comes
Home, I'm On My Way, Spanish Harlem, You Don't Know, Falling In Love With
Love, Who Are We To Say, I Wake Up Cryin'.

Summer Holiday   *January 1963*
Seven Days To A Holiday, Summer Holiday, Let Us Take You For A Ride, Les
Girls, Round and Round, Foot Tapper, Stranger In Town, Orlando's Mime,
Bachelor Boy, A Swingin' Affair, Really Waltzing, All At Once, Dancing Shoes,
Jugoslav Wedding, The Next Time, Big News.

Cliff's Hit Album   *July 1963*
Move It, Living Doll, Travellin' Light, A Voice In The Wilderness, Fall In Love
With You, Please Don't Tease, Nine Time Out Of Ten, I Love You, Theme For A
Dream, A Girl Like You, When The Girl In Your Arms, The Young Ones, I'm
Looking Out The Window, Do You Want To Dance.

When In Spain   *September 1963*
Perfidia, Amor Amor Amor, Frenesi, You Belong To My Heart, Vaya Con Dios,
Sweet & Gentle, Maria No Mas, Miss, Perhaps Perhaps Perhaps, Magic Is The
Moonlight, Carnival, Sway.

Wonderful Life   *July 1964*
Wonderful Life, A Girl in Every Port, Walkin', A Little Imagination, Home, On The
Beach, In The Stars, We Love A Movie, Do You Remember, What've I Gotta Do,
Theme For Young Lovers, All Kinds Of People, A Matter Of Moments, Youth And
Experience.

Aladdin And His Wonderful Lamp   *December 1964*
Emperor Theme, Chinese Street Scene, Me Oh My, I Could Easily Fall (In Love
With You), Little Princess, This Was My Special Day, I'm In Love With You,
There's Gotta Be A Way, Ballet: (Rubies, Emeralds, Sapphires, Diamonds), Dance
Of The Warriors, Friends, Dragon Dance, Genie With The Light Brown Lamp,
Make Ev'ry Day A Carnival Day, Widow Twankey's Song, I'm Feeling Oh So
Lovely, I've Said Too Many Things, Evening Comes, Havin' Fun.

Cliff Richard   *April 1965*
Angel, Sway, I Only Came To Say Goodbye, Take Special Care, Magic Is The
Moonlight, House Without Windows, Razzle Dazzle, I Don't Wanna Love You,
It's Not For Me To Say, You Belong To My Heart, Again, Perfidia, Kiss, Reelin'
And Rockin'.

More Hits – By Cliff   *July 1965*
It'll Be Me, The Next Time, Bachelor Boy, Summer Holiday, Dancing Shoes,
Lucky Lips, It's All In The Game, Don't Talk To Him, I'm The Lonely One,
Constantly, On The Beach, A Matter Of Moments, The Twelfth Of Never, I Could
Easily Fall (In Love With You).

When In Rome   *August 1965*
Come Prima, Volare, Autumn Concerto, The Questions, Maria's Her Name, Don't
Talk To Him, Just Say I Love Her, Arrivederci Roma, A Little Grain Of Sand,
House Without Windows, Che Cosa Del Farai Mio Amore, Me You're Mine.

Love Is Forever   *November 1965*
Everyone Needs Someone To Love, Long Ago And Far Away, All Of A Sudden My
Heart Sings, Have I Told You Lately That I Love You, Fly Me To The Moon, A
Summer Place, I Found A Rose, My Foolish Heart, Through The Eye Of A Needle,
My Colouring Book, I Walk Alone, Someday (You'll Want Me To Want You),
Paradise Lost, Look Homeward Angel.

Kinda Latin   *May 1966*
Blame It On The Bossa Nova, Blowing In The Wind, Quiet Nights Of Quiet Stars, Eso Beso, The Girl From Ypanema, One Note Samba, Fly Me To The Moon, Our Day Will Come, Quando Quando Quando, Come Closer To Me, Meditation, Concrete And Clay.

Finders Keepers   *December 1966*
Finders Keepers, Time Drags By, Washerwoman, La La La Song, My Way, Oh Senorita, Spanish Music, Fiesta, This Day, Paella, Finders Keepers, My Way, Paella, Fiesta, Run To The Door, Where Did The Summer Go, Into Each Life Some Rain Must Fall.

Cinderella   *January 1967*
Welcome To Stoneybroke, Why Wasn't I Born Rich, Peace And Quiet, The Flyder And The Spy, Poverty, The Hunt, In The Country, Come Sunday, Dare I Love Him Like I Do, If Our Dreams Come True, Autumn, The King's Place, Peace And Quiet, She Needs Him More Than Me, Hey Doctor Man.

Don't Stop Me Now   *April 1967*
Shout, One Fine Day, I'll Be Back, Heartbeat, I Saw Her Standing There, Hang On To A Dream, You Gotta Tell Me, Homeward Bound, Good Golly Miss Molly, Don't Make Promises, Move It, Don't, Dizzy Miss Lizzy, Baby It's You, My Babe, Save The Last Dance For Me.

Good News   *October 1967*
Good News, It Is No Secret, We Shall Be Changed, 23rd Psalm, Go Where I Send Thee, What A Friend We Have In Jesus, All Glory Laud And Honour, Just A Closer Walk With Thee, The King Of Love My Shepherd Is, Mary What You Gonna Name That Pretty Little Baby, When I Survey The Wondrous Cross, Take My Hand Precious Lord, Get On Board Little Children, May The Good Lord Bless And Keep You.

Cliff In Japan   *May 1968*
Shout, I'll Come Runnin', The Minute You're Gone, On The Beach, Hang On To A Dream, Spanish Harlem, Finders Keepers, Visions, Evergreen Tree, What'd I Say, Dynamite, Medley: Let's Make A Memory, The Young Ones, Lucky Lips, Summer Holiday, We Say Yeah.

Two A Penny   *August 1968*
Two A Penny, I'll Love You Forever Today, Questions, Long Is The Night, Lonely Girl, And Me (I'm On The Outside Now), Daybreak, Twist And Shout, Celeste. Not from the film: Wake Up Wake Up, Cloudy, Red Rubber Ball, Close To Kathy, Rattler.

Established 1958   *September 1968*
Don't Forget To Catch Me, Voyage To The Bottom Of The Bath, Not The Way That It Should Be, Poem, The Dreams I Dream, The Average Life Of A Daily Man, Somewhere By The Sea, Banana Man, Girl On The Bus, The Magical Mrs Clamps, Ooh La La, Here I Go Again Loving You, What's Behind The Eyes Of Mary, Maggie's Samba.

The Best Of Cliff   *June 1969*
The Minute You're Gone, On My Word, The Time In Between, Wind Me Up (Let
Me Go), Blue Turns To Grey, Visions, Time Drags By, In The Country, It's All
Over, I'll Come Runnin', The Day I Met Marie, All My Love, Congratulations, Girl
You'll Be A Woman Soon.

Sincerely   *October 1969*
In The Past, Always, Will You Love Me Tomorrow, You'll Want Me, I'm Not
Getting Married, Time, For Emily Whenever I May Find Her, Baby I Could Be So
Good At Loving You, Sam, London's Not Too Far, Take Action, Take Good Care
Of Her, When I Find You, Punch & Judy.

It'll Be Me   *November 1969*
It'll Be Me, So I've Been Told, How Long Is Forever, I'm Walkin' The Blues, Turn
Around, Blueberry Hill, Let's Make A Memory, When My Dream Boat Comes
Home, I'm On My Way, Spanish Harlem, You Don't Know, Falling In Love With
Love, Who Are We To Say, I Wake Up Cryin'.

Cliff Live At The Talk Of The Town   *July 1970*
Introduction Congratulations, Shout, All My Love, Ain't Nothing But A House
Party, Something Good/If Ever I Should Leave You, Girl You'll Be A Woman Soon,
Hank's Medley: London's Not Too Far, The Dreams I Dream, The Day I Met
Marie, La La La La La, A Taste Of Honey, The Lady Came From Baltimore, When
I'm 64, What's More I Don't Need Her, Bows & Fanfare, Congratulations, Visions,
Finale Congratulations.

About That Man   *October 1970*
The Birth Of John The Baptist, Sweet Little Jesus Boy, The Visit Of The Wise Men
And The Escape To Egypt, John The Baptist Points Out Jesus, Jesus Recruits His
Helpers And Heals The Sick, Where Is That Man, Jesus Addresses The Crowd On
The Hill-Side, Can It Be True, Jesus Is Betrayed And Arrested, The Trial Of Jesus,
His Execution And Death, The First Easter – The Empty Tomb, Reflections.

His Land   *November 1970*
Ezekiel's Vision, Dry Bones, His Land, Jerusalem, Jerusalem, The New 23rd,
His Land, Hava Nagila, Over In Bethlehem, Keep Me Where Love Is, He's
Everything To Me, Narration And Hallelujah Chorus.

Tracks 'n Grooves   *November 1970*
Early In The Morning, As I Walk Into The Morning Of Your Life, Love Truth &
Emily Stone, My Head Goes Around, Put My Mind At Ease, Abraham, Martin &
John, The Girl Can't Help It, Bang Bang (My Baby Shot Me Down), I'll Make It All
Up To You, I'd Just Be Fool Enough, Don't Let Tonight Ever End, What A Silly
Thing To Do, Your Heart's Not In Your Love, Don't Ask Me To Be Friends, Are
You Only Fooling Me.

The Best Of Cliff Volume Two   *November 1972*
Goodbye Sam, Hello Samantha, Marianne, Throw Down A Line, Jesus, Sunny Honey Girl, I Ain't Got Time Anymore, Flying Machine, Sing A Song Of Freedom, With The Eyes Of A Child, Good Times, I'll Love You Forever Today, The Joy Of Living, Silvery Rain, Big Ship.

Take Me High   *December 1973*
It's Only Monday, Midnight Blue, Hover (Instrumental), Why (Duet with Anthony Andrews), Life, Driving, The Game, Brumburger Duet (Duet with Debbie Watling), Take Me High, The Anti-Brotherhood Of Man, Winning, Driving (Instrumental), Join The Band, The Word Is Love, Brumburger (Finale).

Help It Along   *June 1974*
Day By Day, Celestial Houses, Jesus, Silvery Rain, Jesus Loves You, Fire And Rain, Yesterday Today Forever, Mr. Business Man, Help It Along, Amazing Grace, Higher Ground, Sing A Song Of Freedom.

The 31st Of February Street   *November 1974*
31st Of February Street Opening, Give Me Back That Old Familiar Feeling, The Leaving, Travellin' Light, There You Go Again, Nothing To Remind Me, Our Love Could Be So Real, No Matter What, Fireside Song, Going Away, Long Long Time, You Will Never Know, The Singer, 31st of February Street Closing.

I'm Nearly Famous   *May 1976*
I Can't Ask For Anymore Than You, It's No Use Pretending, I'm Nearly Famous, Lovers, Junior Cowboy, Miss You Nights, I Wish You'd Change Your Mind, Devil Woman, Such Is The Mystery, You've Got To Give Me All Your Lovin', Alright, It's Alright.

Every Face Tells A Story   *March 1977*
My Kinda Life, Must Be Love, When Two Worlds Drift Apart, You Got Me Wondering, Every Face Tells A Story (It Never Tells A Lie), Try A Smile, Hey Mr. Dream Maker, Give Me Love Your Way, Up In The World, Don't Turn The Light Out, It'll Be Me Babe, Spider Man.

40 Golden Greats   *September 1977*
Move It, Livin' Doll, Travellin' Light, Fall In Love With You, Please Don't Tease, Nine Times Out Of Ten, Theme For A Dream, Gee Whizz It's You, When The Girl In Your Arms Is The Girl In Your Heart, A Girl Like You, The Young Ones, Do You Want To Dance? I'm Lookin' Out The Window, It'll Be Me, Bachelor Boy, The Next Time, Summer Holiday, Lucky Lips, It's All In The Game, Don't Talk To Him, Constantly, On The Beach, I Could Easily Fall (In Love With You), The Minute You're Gone, Wind Me Up (Let Me Go), Visions, Blue Turns To Grey, In The Country, The Day I Met Marie, All My Love, Congratulations, Throw Down A Line, Goodbye Sam Hello Samantha, Sing A Song Of Freedom, Power To All Our Friends, (You Keep Me) Hangin' On, Miss You Nights, Devil Woman, I Can't Ask For Anymore Than You, My Kinda Life.

Small Corners   *February 1978*
Why Should The Devil Have All The Good Music, I Love, Why Me, I've Got News
For You, Hey Whatcha' Say, I Wish We'd All Been Ready, Joseph, Good On The
Sally Army, Goin' Home, Up In Canada, Yes He Lives, When I Survey The
Wondrous Cross.

Bill Latham

AFTER A FRIENDSHIP of fourteen years and involvement in Cliff's conversion to Christ in 1965, few people know Cliff Richard as closely as Bill Latham.

He was born in North London in 1938 and, following school, worked for three years as a journalist with the Barnet Press. Indulging a growing desire to teach, he then studied Divinity and English at Trent Park Training College in Barnet, before taking up a post as Head of Religious Education at Riversmead School, Cheshunt. It was during his eight years there that he first met Cliff Richard, whose sister, Joan, was a pupil at the school.

In 1970 he was appointed Education Officer at TEAR (The Evangelical Alliance Relief) Fund, a London-based Christian relief and development organisation, and was its Deputy Director between 1973 and 1978. In this connection, he travelled widely, both in the UK and abroad.

For the past thirteen years he has found time to help steer Cliff Richard's Christian ministry, to organise his programme of Christian engagements, and to appear with him in Christian dialogue sessions throughout Britain and often overseas. He now more formally directs Cliff's charity trust company, which is the 'umbrella' organisation for all Cliff's Christian and non-commercial activities.

*Front cover photograph/*Peter Vernon
Designed by Bob Hook